Informal Teaching and Learning
A Study of Everyday Cognition
in a Greek Community

Informal Teaching and Learning
A Study of Everyday Cognition
in a Greek Community

Rosemary C. Henze
Art, Research, & Curriculum Associates
Oakland, CA

 LAWRENCE ERLBAUM ASSOCIATES, PUBLISHERS
1992   Hillsdale, New Jersey   Hove and London

Lawrence Erlbaum Associates, Inc., Publishers
365 Broadway
Hillsdale, New Jersey 07642

Cover photo by Panos Panagos, 1991

Library of Congress Cataloging-in-Publication Data
Henze, Rosemary.
   Informal teaching and learning : a study of everyday cognition in
a Greek community / Rosemary Henze.
      p. /n/n cm.
   Includes bibliographical references (p.   ) and index.
   ISBN 0-8058-0988-0
   1. Non-formal education--Greece. 2. Cognition and culture-
-Greece. 3. Educational anthropology--Greece. I. Title.
LC45.8.G8H46   1992
370.19--dc20   91-23940
                                                       CIP
Printed in the United States of America
10   9   8   7   6   5   4   3   2   1

.

To my sister *Claire*
and in memory of
Giorgos Nestoras Panagos

Contents

Preface

This book honors the particulars of everyday life. Based on an ethnographic study conducted in a Greek community, it celebrates the small ways people teach and learn while they are engaged in other, supposedly more important, activities. By examining the intricate ways in which knowledge and skills of everyday life are transmitted, I hope to show how family, community, and culture shape the cognitive world of learners.

My decision to study informal teaching and learning in Greece, while it had its academic origins, was also motivated by personal curiosity. Over many years of interacting with Greeks both in Greece and in the United States, I had wondered how learning processes might be different for Greeks than for Americans of northern European backgrounds such as myself. An example of an event that whetted this curiosity was a party I attended in San Francisco for a Greek friend's name day. Most of the people attending the party were in their 20s and 30s and were or had been at one time foreign students in the United States. Some had since become permanent residents or citizens, but all shared direct roots in Greece. One young man brought with him his aunt, a woman in her 50s, who had just arrived from Greece for an extended visit. When the dancing began (as it almost always did at such gatherings), it became clear that the aunt was an expert dancer. She led several circle dances with great finesse, wheeling and turning and generally doing what Greeks call *figoures* — special moves by the lead dancer involving more creativity and skill than the regular dance steps done by the others in the circle. When an American woman indicated to her that she wanted to learn, the aunt took her by the hand and brought her firmly into the circle. Pulling the American woman along, the aunt continued to dance as an expert does, her only accommodation to the learner being perhaps a slightly heavier stress on downbeats.

Watching the American woman's confused feet and puzzled, frustrated facial expressions, I realized that she and I shared certain expectations about how one teaches another person to dance that were not being met. We expected the dance steps to be broken down into simpler components, but the aunt was doing nothing of the sort. She expected the American woman to "learn by doing"—perhaps not the first time, but cumulatively over successive events. On many occasions since then I have observed similar forms of instruction in which learners do not appear to be "instructed" in a step-by-step process but rather become participants in activities with experts, and through modeling and observation, they eventually learn. Although this formulation of the differences turned out to be only the tip of a much larger iceberg, it was enough to motivate further, more careful, exploration.

This book is the result of that exploration. It is of interest to educational researchers, cognitive anthropologists, cognitive psychologists, and cultural anthropologists as each in their own ways seek answers to questions about the interaction of culture and learning. Educational researchers, who have traditionally focused their studies on formal schooling, are finding that informal education has been ignored too long. Not only are formal and informal instruction more closely linked than we previously thought, but informal instruction can tell us a great deal about culturally specific ways of teaching and learning. As schools in the United States and other technologically advanced nations grow more and more culturally diverse, educators who are accustomed to teaching children of similar cultural backgrounds to their own are becoming aware (often painfully) that successful instruction for one population does not necessarily work for children of very different backgrounds. Increasingly, educators turn to anthropology to explore how schooling can be made more "culturally relevant" to children of diverse backgrounds, and many schools of education now require prospective teachers to take a course in "multicultural education" in order to better meet the needs of their future students (Banks & Banks 1989).

Cognitive anthropologists and cognitive psychologists will also find material of interest here, for the book provides detailed descriptions of the processes through which specific cultural content is taught and learned. Vygotsky's theory of the social origins of cognition (1962, 1978), which has led many researchers to rethink earlier paradigms of cognitive development, is both exemplified and re-examined. The teaching and learning processes that I describe are firmly situated in everyday task environments that are shaped by the local culture as well as by the dynamics of time, place, and participants. Finally, cultural anthropologists specializing in the Mediterranean, or Greece in particular, will find that the book addresses questions of cultural transmission through an exploration of the theme of struggle (*aghona*) and the ways in which this theme is taught, learned, and continually created anew.

My entry to the community of Kiriakitsa,[1] where I lived and carried out most of my observations, was made possible by my earlier experiences there. I first visited the community in 1978, when I traveled to Greece with my husband to meet his parents, Grigoris and Katerina Yorgakis, and the rest of his family. I had already learned enough of the language to communicate adequately with my in-laws, a fact we all valued. We visited the community once again in 1981, and in 1983 we were divorced. I continued, however, to maintain communication with the family in Greece; they seemed to want this continuing relationship, and I did too. In 1985, I discussed with both my ex-husband and his family the advisability of going to the village to do my doctoral research for 8 months and living with family members during this time. Everyone accepted, and so I made my plans and arrived to begin fieldwork on April 26, 1986—in time for Greek Easter and the upheaval of the Chernobyl explosion.

Just as the learning I studied was social in origin, so too, was the process that led to this book. I am grateful to everyone who helped me. Without the acceptance and support of my Greek family, otherwise known distantly as "the informants," this study would not have been possible. I have not used their real names because of human subjects policy, but they know who they are. As I watched the videotapes over and over again, I always felt a sense of wonder, and often sadness that I cannot live two lives—one with them, and one in the world I now inhabit. Then I remind myself that I carry them with me to the extent that I have internalized their ways of seeing things, their voices. I hope the book gives readers a sense of how these people honored me with their acceptance.

Panos, my former husband, was a crucial link between the idea and its realization. He has always encouraged me in my work, and I could not have carried out the study without his full agreement. I am also grateful to him for helping me fill in missing information when I began analyzing and interpreting the data. Finally, my fluency in the Greek language, and particularly in the regional dialect, originated in the years we spent together.

My dissertation advisor, Thom Huebner, participated in the very beginning of the idea during a brainstorming session in which he had the wisdom to tell me when I had discovered a workable topic. During fieldwork, when I was so immersed in community life that I tended to forget the academic world, his correspondence helped me to keep a sense of perspective, reminding me that the world in which dissertations meant something still

---

[1]The names of the village and the informants have been fictionalized.

existed. As a linguist, his comments helped shape my analyses of the discourse of informal teaching and learning.

Chuck Frake, who was also on my dissertation committee, provided the perspective of a cognitive anthropologist, and Fred Erickson, who was willing to be a member of my committee from across the country, gave valuable input on the sociolinguistics of face-to-face interaction and the use and analysis of video recordings. Shirley Brice Heath, Lee Shulman, and George Spindler also read and commented on early and late versions of the dissertation.

I thank my parents, Katherine and Robert Henze, for fostering my formal and informal education in ways that prepared me to complete this study. My sister Claire, to whom this book is dedicated, offered me an inside view of informal teaching and learning in an American family. Although the study does not explicitly draw on this contrast, I have nonetheless learned much from observing her interactions with her children, Nicholas and Anna.

Many friends and colleagues have given me helpful suggestions and moral support. Tamara Lucas, whose career has paralleled mine for the past 14 years, has been my closest ally throughout this process, always willing to encourage me as well as to commiserate with me. Palle Henckel helped me prepare for fieldwork by advising me about videocameras, transcribers, transformers, and all the other machinery I took. Popi Spanou and Elene Exarhou transcribed many hours of audiotape—a boring task at best, but one they did cheerfully, with an excellent sense of the finer details of everyday talk. Hervé Varenne's comments guided me in moving from dissertation to book, and Hollis Heimbouch and Robin Weisberg at Lawrence Erlbaum Associates provided sensitive editing assistance. Sau Lim Tsang, executive director of ARC Associates, generously allowed me to use ARC's facilities to complete the manuscript.

Finally, my husband Joseph Grieco has been loving and supportive from the time he met me in 1987, when I was analyzing the data, to this past year in which he has intimately observed the reframing of the study in book form. He cooked wonderful meals for me when I would have otherwise survived on instant soup, and in many other ways stands as evidence that nurturing comes easily to some men.

To all of you, many thanks.

Rosemary C. Henze

1 How to Ring a Doorbell

September 17, 1986. On a warm afternoon in the village of Kiriakitsa, 4-year-old Alexis tags along as his grandfather, Grigoris, waters the fruit trees around the house. As they approach the front of the house, Alexis looks toward the door: "The doorbell!" (*To koudhouni!*),[1] he says with excitement and runs lightly up the marble steps to the door, reaching up toward the bell.

"You don't reach" (*Dhen ftans*), says Grigoris, nearing the steps and putting his hands on his hips as he watches his grandchild. "You don't reach" (*Dhen ftaneis*), he repeats, this time in more standard Greek. By now Alexis is climbing onto a chair in order to reach the bell.

"I do reach, I get up here" (*Ftano, anevaino edho pano*), he counters.

"Let me see" (*Yia na dho*), says the grandfather, and then, as he sees Alexis reach up somewhat precariously from the chair, "Don't fall" (*Mi paiseis*).

"And if I fall?" (*Kai a'ma paiso;*).[2] The child reaches to press the bell. Nothing happens.

"It didn't hit" (*Dhen varese*).

"I reach" (*Ftano*), insists Alexis as he gets down from the chair.

---

[1] In the transliteration of Greek, I have tried to capture as closely as possible the way people actually pronounce the language, including dialectical variations. Most of the transliteration is based on repeated review of audio and videotapes.

[2] In the Greek version, following the conventions of written Greek, I have used semicolons to indicate questions.

"It didn't ring, I mean" (*Dhen ktipise, na poume*), Grigoris says as he walks up the steps to where Alexis is standing and indicates the chair: "Get up here" (*Aneva edho pano*).

Alexis repeats this as he climbs, "I get up here, sh sh sh" (*Anevo edho pano, sh sh sh*).

"It will ring a lot though, right?" (*Tha ktipai poli omos, etsi;*), says the grandfather.

"Aaah?"

"You'll ring a lot" (*Tha ktipeis poli*).

"I ring a lot" (*Ktipiso poli*), Alexis repeats as he reaches for the bell.

"Wait" (*Stasou*). Grigoris holds out his hand as if to stop Alexis, but instead reaches to press the doorbell himself. "They don't ring here . . . here, like this" (*Dhen patane edho . . . edho, etsi*). The first sound of the doorbell coincides exactly with the stressed second syllable in the word *edho* (here). Then Grigoris moves his hand away, allowing Alexis' finger to press the bell.

A resounding ring is heard this time, and another, and simultaneously an outpouring of words: "And now—I'll press the bell and I'll shake up all—I'll sha—I'll I'll shake up all the neighborhood!" (*Kai tora—tha patiso to koudhouni kai tha vrondiso olo—tha vron—tha tha vrondiso oli tin yitonyia!*).

The door opens from inside, and Alexis' grandmother Katerina appears. "Let go—Grandma's here" (*As—irthe i yiayia*), says Grigoris.

Alexis rings the bell again.

"Won't you tell me" (*Dhen mou les*), says Katerina, "Won't you tell me, ah, don't touch there [the bell] you bad boy" (*Dhen mou les, ah, mi patas aftou, paliopaido*).

Grigoris and Alexis both laugh.

"Ah hah—a spanking—you'll ruin it, the bell" (*Ah hah—ksilo—tha to halaseis to koudhouni*), laughs Katerina as she playfully boxes her grandson's head.

"I'll ruin it, what will I do" (*Tha to halaso, ti to kano*), challenges Alexis.

"I'll take yours from you" (*Tha sou paro to dhiko sou*), she teases as she slides her hand up the front of his t-shirt and tweaks his nipple. Grandmother and grandson exchange mock threats in this manner for a few moments until Grigoris intervenes:

"Come on, stop now, get down" (*Ela, stamata tora, kateva*).

"Quiet" (*Isihia*), adds Alexis, as he climbs down from the chair.

"Quiet please" (*Isihia parakalo*), repeats Katerina, returning indoors.[3]

---

[3]This scene was transcribed from videotape. The vignette attempts to convey the interplay of both verbal and nonverbal interaction.

Figure 1. Alexis receives instruction from Grigoris in ringing the doorbell.

INTRODUCTION TO THE STUDY

The scene just described took place in a Greek village located in the central plains of Thessaly. Although unique in its context, participants, and dialogue, this teaching and learning episode also exemplifies many of the characteristics that make informal teaching and learning a compelling subject to study. In this scene Alexis, who knows a good deal about ringing the doorbell at his parents' home, experiences some trouble applying what he already knows about doorbells to a different situation. This doorbell is higher than the one at his parents' home, and ringing it requires a different amount of pressure. The first time he tries, nothing happens. After some verbal and nonverbal help from his grandfather, however, Alexis rings the bell three times. His flurry of talk after the second and third rings indicates his pleasure in this success, and his grandmother's appearance at the door completes the sequence of summons and response that is expected in the adult world. Following that, the grandmother and grandchild oppose each other in a teasing manner characteristic of many interactions in this community and others in Greece.

Scenes of informal teaching and learning such as the one described here are both fleeting and commonplace in the lives of most children. The entire process described transpired in less than a minute, and hundreds of interactions such as this occur in a child's day. Perhaps because of the evanescent qualities of informal teaching and learning and the difficulty of capturing it in natural settings, it is rarely documented and studied.

The interaction of Alexis and his grandparents bears only partial resemblance to what we typically think of as education, for it lacks many of the features we associate with schooling. Without a formal opening (e.g., "class is beginning now") and formal closing (e.g., "that's all for today"), without the kind of overt evaluation we have come to expect (e.g., "very good, Johnny"), it may at first glance seem irrelevant to educators. Yet it is not difficult to recognize in the interaction a teacher, Grigoris; a learner, Alexis; and a subject matter, ringing the doorbell. In short, this is a scene of informal education, which LaBelle (1984) defined as "the education of daily living," differentiating it from institutionalized, chronologically ordered, or organized instruction.

In the past, descriptions of the teaching and learning that go on in everyday life outside of schools have been largely the realm of anthropologists and to some extent sociolinguists interested in children's language development. The relative lack of interest in informal learning on the part of the education community can be explained in several ways. First, most researchers in education take it as their duty to seek understanding of and solutions to problems of formal education manifested largely in schools. They assume that if the problem is located in school, then understanding and resolution of that problem require research in school. Second, trouble in schools carries with it a sense of urgency, often heightened by economic and political debate; this urgency provides another reason for educational research to focus on schools. And third, even those who see the value of looking beyond school are often discouraged by the special methodological problems of doing research in everyday environments, where one cannot isolate variables and where "proof" must be replaced by a more realistic goal, "the demonstration of plausibility." (Erickson, 1986a, p.136)

Attitudes about the marginality of informal education are reflected in the very vocabulary used to classify types of education—formal, nonformal, and informal. Formal education takes on the normative status, whereas nonformal and informal appear, in their morphology at least, to be variants of this norm. Historically, however, formal schooling is the variant and informal education the norm, for mass formal schooling occupies less than a century in the history and prehistory of the human race (Coleman, 1987). Studying informal teaching and learning in its natural contexts can tell us a great deal about the intricate ways in which knowledge and skills of everyday life are transmitted and about the influence of family, community, and culture on the early education of children.

This study was guided by two broad research questions:

1. What makes informal teaching and learning episodes as a class similar to one another and different from the stream of activity surrounding them?
2. How do informal teaching and learning vary in a community in central Greece, and what, if any, are the consequences of such variation for the learner?

The first question seeks unity; it asks how a great variety of activities can nonetheless share certain common features we call teaching and learning. The second question seeks within that unity for the differences among types, leaving open the question of which differences will be most salient.

As I set out to identify and describe informal teaching and learning in the context of Greek family and community life, several key conceptual issues arose. The rest of this chapter is devoted to addressing these issues. I begin with culture, the overarching framework, then move to more specific questions of definition and analytical categories, and finally back to the broader question of how frames of interpretation affect the teaching and learning process.

THE ROLE OF CULTURE

At the heart of this study lies the question of how culture—in this case, the culture of a Greek community in Thessaly—influences processes of teaching and learning and how these processes in turn shape or reinforce culture. Because all human interaction is embedded in cultural contexts, instruction in homes and communities reflects the culturally constructed ways of behaving of a particular family and their social environment, just as instruction in school reflects the "culture of the school," which encourages certain ways of speaking and behaving and discourages others. In addition to this reflective quality, face-to-face interaction also actively constructs, modifies, and negotiates cultural patterns, for culture is not static. Rather, it is constantly being re-interpreted and modified by people in interaction.

I also assume that culture is both internal and external. It is not only embodied in collective rituals and everyday practices but also in the minds of individuals. It is what one has to know in order to behave appropriately in a given community (Goodenough, 1957). This view of culture, based on the precepts of cognitive anthropology, sees cognition as deeply situated and lends itself to studying both external and internal aspects of culture.

Although culture has always been an important construct in education, educators in the 20th century have shifted in the the roles they assign to culture. We have seen a movement from culture and race as biological determinants of intelligence (and hence educability) to a "cultural deficit" model that claimed minority children did poorly in school because they lacked "culture," to the recent understanding that all children bring rich cultural backgrounds to the school, some of which are valued by the school and some of which are not. Research on situated cognition enables us to specify with greater accuracy what is universal about learning and what is context and culture dependent.

Knowledge of the interaction of culture with teaching and learning can help educators understand the school performance of diverse student populations. When educators discuss why certain children consistently fail at school, they frequently invoke cultural difference as a source of difficulty. Anthropologists and sociolinguists have done a great deal to uncover possible cultural factors influencing children in school, but much remains to be done. A number of studies have explored ways in which informal practices in the homes of minority as well as mainstream children "carry over" in school. When these practices, which may consist of a communicative style, a particular social participation structure, or a way of organizing narratives, are similar to those expected in school, "cultural congruence" is said to exist between the home and school environments. When, on the other hand, practices in the home differ from practices in the school, then the home and school environments are said to be culturally incongruent. This incongruity can result in cognitive dissonance, making it more difficult for students to do well in school because they must learn not only lesson content but also a different way of interacting (Erickson, 1986a).

Among Athabaskans in Western Canada, for example, elders may repeat or gloss after children's utterances, but they rarely question them or ask for elaborations (Scollon & Scollon, 1981). Patterns such as these, valued in the home, may not be recognized or valued in the school; when this happens, children are placed at a disadvantage compared to their mainstream peers, whose patterns of interaction at home are more similar to those used in school. Teachers, not understanding why certain children cannot seem to master a particular practice expected in class, may treat these children differentially by not involving them as often in classroom talk or by reacting negatively to their attempts to participate. A number of ethnographic studies have attested to similar problems as minority children encounter the school environment (see e.g., Au & Mason, 1983; Delgado-Gaitan, 1987; Gilmore, 1983; Heath, 1983; John, 1972; Levin, 1990; Michaels & Collins, 1984; Michaels & Cook-Gumperz, 1979; Ochs, 1982; Philips, 1972; Schieffelin, 1979).

Understanding the values and priorities that lie behind culturally based discourse styles may also provide insight into informal teaching and learning styles, for the "teaching and learning styles of a particular group reflect the discourse patterns of that group" (Scollon & Scollon, 1981, p.191). For example, both Athabaskan riddle and narrative verse are outcomes of a style of face-to-face interaction that emphasizes indirectness and joint sense-making. This style is reflected outward again in typical patterns of teaching and learning between Athabaskan adults and children. Previous research has assumed that vertical constructions[4] are a universal phenomenon of adult-child discourse leading to the development of syntax. Athabaskans, however, do not use vertical constructions; the adults, rather than asking questions that lead to more elaboration by the child, only gloss after the children's utterances. This led Scollon and Scollon (1984) to suggest that vertical constructions may be an "aspect of careful socialization in the discourse patterns of literacy" (p.182).

The communicative style of Greeks has been studied by Tannen (1984), whose work on the "oral-literate continuum" and conversational style also stresses the priorities that underlie different interactive styles. In an article that compares Greek and American oral and written narratives, she found that the Greek narratives included more interpretation. She concluded that "Interpretation . . . is the way of acknowledging the interpersonal involvement of speaker and hearer to which the spoken mode, and Greek communicative style, are more disposed" (p.34).

Although it is possible in some cases to determine such priorities from discourse alone, often it is necessary to look beyond discourse for these

---

[4]Vertical constructions are those in which a child builds cumulatively upon an adult's framework or scaffold, as in: Child: "Tape recorder, use it, use it." Adult: "Use it for what?" Child: "Talk, corder talk, Brenda talk" (Scollon & Scollon, 1984, p.181).

explanations. Ethnography gives researchers time and experience in the communities they study, enabling them to make connections between discrete events and larger patterns. Friedl (1962), for example, who found that Greek adults in the village of Vasilika teased children a great deal, related this interactional pattern to the larger cultural theme of struggle. Similarly, Scollon and Scollon could not have achieved their understanding of Athabaskan communicative patterns without broader understanding of the beliefs and values of the community, gained through their roles as participant observers. Whenever possible, interpretations of particular discourse features need to be integrated with ethnographic information about the communities we study.

Although cultural differences such as those discussed here can certainly contribute to trouble in school, there is a danger in viewing cultural difference in an overly deterministic way. Cultural difference does not always cause trouble. In the United States, it is the "caste-like" minorities (e.g., African-Americans, Chicanos, Puerto Ricans) who seem to have the most trouble. Immigrant minorities (e.g., Southeast Asians, Punjabis) generally do better in school and are seemingly not at a great disadvantage due to their different backgrounds (Ogbu, 1978). Furthermore, culturally incongruous education can sometimes work very well, even for caste-like minorities. For example, students in Black Muslim schools, Roman Catholic parochial schools with White teachers, and Marva Collins' school in Chicago all seem to do well academically, despite the schools' intentionally *not* incorporating interaction patterns found in the students' homes and communities (Erickson, 1987). Apparently it is not cultural difference per se that always creates trouble. In fact, Varenne and McDermott (1986) pointed out that schooling is structured so that some students *must* fail. The individual does not matter in so far as the school is concerned; if a previously failing student "turns around" and begins to succeed, another "failure" will take that student's place.

Several studies have suggested that trouble in school can amplify cultural difference and foster student resistance to learning. Piestrup (1973) found that when a teacher, whether Black or White, made an issue of African American children's use of the vernacular in class, those children spoke a more exaggerated form of the dialect by the end of the school year. When, on the other hand, the teacher did not negatively sanction the dialect, children came to speak in more standard ways by the end of the year. In this study, a cultural difference in speech patterns became stigmatized by the teacher, and what began perhaps as a simple misinterpretation developed over time into entrenched teacher-student conflict (Erickson, 1987). Bateson (1972) called this ever increasing spiral of conflict "complimentary schizmogenesis."

Greek children are not generally one of the stigmatized groups in U.S.

schools, so this study is not an attempt to remediate failure. It is, however, an attempt to understand how a Greek family and community influence informal learning. If we assume there is a relationship between informal and formal education, this understanding will further our knowledge of the relevance of culture (not only Greek culture) to teaching and learning processes both in and out of school.

SOCIAL NETWORKS

Although culture certainly influences the way informal teaching and learning is carried out, individuals also make their mark. For this reason, it was critical that this study consider who teaches whom, for what reasons, and how often. This led to an examination of social networks in the community where I lived.

The concept of a social network, developed first by Boissevain (1974), has been used to analyze how innovations are spread among members of a community. Most Greek villages are very tightly woven, personalistic social worlds, exemplifying what Boissevain referred to as a "dense" network. Network density is the degree to which, for example, two people known by Individual A also know each other. The relationships in a dense network also tend to be "multiplex"; that is, individuals who know each other tend to have several different relationships simultaneously. They may, for example, be cousins, friends, co-workers, and also husbands of two sisters. On the other hand, certain individuals in the village may have more relationships with people in the "outside" world due to business interests or educational level.

An incident that occured during the fifth month of my fieldwork illustrates the importance of social network in the development of certain social registers. I had traveled for a few days to Thessaloniki, where I met a female pediatrician with whom I discussed my work. She was very helpful and later sent me an article I had asked about. After returning to Kiriakitsa, I wrote her a thank you letter in Greek, but when I came to the closing salutation, I found that my Greek, learned mainly in informal contexts, was not adequate to the task of properly closing a letter to a professional woman I had only met once. I therefore turned to Katerina, a villager in her 60s who had a third-grade education. I explained the situation to her and asked how I should close the letter. "I kiss you with love" (*Se filo me aghapi*), she replied. Somewhat mystified and almost certain that this could not be an appropriate closing, I then asked Katerina's daughter, who ran a beauty shop in town and had a ninth-grade education. "With friendly love" (*Me filiki aghapi*), she suggested. This still seemed overly personal for my note, so I descended another generation and asked Mairi, a 17-year-old girl who was studying for her university entrance exams. "With respect" (*Me ektimisi*), she replied. Needless to say, I chose this ending for my letter.

Their different answers serve as reminders of the changing functions of letter writing in these women's lives and the audiences whom they address in writing. Katerina's and Anna's responses indicate that they have little to no experience with writing letters to strangers or near-strangers. They responded to my question with the only closings they knew, which were for personal friends and relatives. Mairi's answer, on the other hand, is appropriate to situations in which one writes to strangers or near-strangers. Although she has yet to really enter the public world, Mairi is being prepared in school for a life in which she has to communicate in writing with a range of different people outside her own personal world.

During the 8 months of fieldwork, I documented 109 instances of indigenous informal teaching and learning. Certainly many more occurred, but these are the ones for which I have records on audiotape, videotape, or in fieldnotes.[5] Appendix A shows the types of variation I looked at and the number of episodes in each category. What is most telling is that a large percentage of the episodes I documented took place among people in the same social network (88%). This does not mean that *interaction* across networks does not occur in Kiriakitsa and Trikala, but it does tell us that informal teaching and learning are not likely to occur across networks.

INFORMAL AND FORMAL

The focus on informal education in this study might be construed as an absence of attention to formal education. However, formality is critical to an understanding of informality because each is relative to the other. In fact, the data show that informal teaching, which to many implies a lack of structure, actually involves considerable structure. In a study of tailor's apprentices in Liberia, Lave (1982) made a similar point, exposing the rules and regularities of the supposedly informal apprenticeship process. Interestingly, the definitions of three levels of formality that LaBelle proposed rest primarily on differences in setting rather than educational process. Formal education, according to LaBelle (1984), is institutionalized and has a defined curriculum; informal education is "the education of daily living"

---

[5]I actually started with 168, but eliminated 28 because they did not hold up under closer examination as teaching and learning. They included instances of getting information, giving directives, and other speech acts that in and of themselves do not constitute informal teaching and learning. Of the 140 that remained, 109 were indigenous, and 31 were nonindigenous. That is, they were initiated by the researcher or the researcher played a major role as teacher or learner.

outside of school; and nonformal education is organized but does not take place in institutions.[6]

Formality, according to Irvine (1979), can be determined by examining the social setting, the communicative code, and in some cases the analyst's description. Because these three dimensions co-occur so often, they are often confused and collapsed as though they were all one phenomenon. For example, a formal social setting such as a job interview normally co-occurs with a formal way of speaking; when such an event is described by an analyst, the description too tends to be formal. However, it is possible to have an informal chat even within this formal social setting or to describe a formal event in an informal way.

This mixing of styles occurs in classrooms too. At its most formal, classroom interaction may consist of repetitive sequences in which a teacher initiation (I) is followed by a student response (R), which is in turn followed by a teacher evaluation of the response (E). Whole lessons are frequently structured around "IRE" sequences, one after another (Mehan, 1979). But although this highly structured, formal participation pattern may be characteristic of many classrooms, it does not adequately describe the range of formality levels possible in school. For example, in one study of a bilingual special education classroom, three kinds of activity exhibited different levels of formality, from relatively informal sociodramatic play, to rather formal lessons and very formal class openings (Ruiz, 1988). The level of formality also varies with the teacher, some teachers preferring a more informal structure (Dickenson, 1985). Classroom instruction contains these informal sequences because, like instruction outside of school, it is carried out through face-to-face interaction that requires improvising as well as rule following. Ideally, there is give and take between formal and informal systems such that the stress of performing according to a formal code is relieved by informality in another area, thus building into educational environments a "wiggle" in much the same way engineers do when they build bridges (Erickson, 1986b; personal communication, February 8, 1988). Thus, it is an oversimplification to assume that classroom teaching is always entirely formal.

Irvine suggested that the discourse aspects and the situational aspects of formality be broken down further to the following variables:

1. increased code structuring,
2. code consistency,
3. invoking positional identities, and
4. emergence of a central situational focus.

---

[6]Grassroots education such as the literacy movement organized by Paolo Freire in Brazil exemplifies what Labelle referred to as nonformal education.

To illustrate, let us turn to another episode that was recorded early in my fieldwork in Greece. In this scene a grown-up daughter makes bread with her mother, and at my request because I was going to be away that day, tapes the interaction. Because she had said she was going to use a new method, I had asked her to talk through the process as though her mother were her student. In other words, I had asked her to contrive a teaching and learning episode for me, and she complied. The result was instructive in several ways. I learned quickly that this was *not* the way to collect examples of indigenous teaching and learning, for by making this request, I instigated an event that never would have happened otherwise. But beyond this, the interaction between daughter and mother shows rather clearly how constituents of formality come to be added as an event takes on a more formal tone.

The daughter's sense of the audience that would listen to the tape was probably a major determinant of formality. She knew that the tape would return with me to *Ameriki*, and she assumed that unknown Americans would listen to it (or read a translation at least). In order to communicate with this perceived audience, she used a repetitive intonation pattern for her teaching as well as slower, louder, clearer speech. She also used lexical items that would not occur in her everyday speech, such as *en sineheia* (in continuance) when she had already used the less formal word *meta* (after). The breadmaking did not progress very far before the interaction split off into two sequences, one public (for the recorder) and the other private. Whispered conversation between mother and daughter, not intended for the tape recorder, formed a kind of backstage communication where the real work of breadmaking was done. The daughter moved back and forth between the structured "show" strand and the "everyday" strand, whereas the mother, less concerned with the show, kept her communication quiet and informal.

One can explain the semi-formality of this episode as an effect of my imposition on the everyday activity of the informants. The episode was false in that the informants did not believe in the roles they had taken on. The mother had baked bread thousands of times more than the daughter, and thus she rejected the role of learner and made the daughter's continuing "teacher" role appear almost ridiculous.

The breadbaking episode shows several features of formality, including increased code structuring such as the daughter's slower, clearer speech and use of more formal vocabulary. It also shows the emergence of a central situational focus. According to Irvine, this focusing emerges in its strongest and clearest form when a large number of participants are present at a gathering such as a lecture, where there is a main sequence that is meant to concern the whole gathering and various side sequences in which topic and relevance are less constrained. Although this episode involves no large audience, breadmaking emerges as the central focus, whereas other topics appear only in whispered asides.

The elements of formality in this scene no doubt emerged because the instruction was not indigenous. However, there were other occasions when features of formality emerged through indigenous participation, for example when a father played a game with his two sons modeled after a TV quiz show. He repeatedly framed questions whose answers he knew, and the structuring of these questions was quite consistent (e.g., "Now. Which child can tell us . . . ?").

An early finding was that although the teaching and learning I studied was as a whole informal, the degree of informality varied. Thus, a small percentage (15%) of the episodes I documented did show some of the features of formality discussed by Irvine.[7] These episodes typically involved activities related to the larger world outside of immediate family life — activities such as going to a lecture on radiation after the Chernobyl explosion, preparing for the Panhellenic Exams, playing school, and playing the questioning game that was probably derived from a television quiz show. These data support the work of others who have found the formal/informal distinction too dichotomous. They suggest instead a continuum from formal to informal educational processes and point to the existence of some features of formality in everyday teaching and learning.

SETTING BOUNDARIES

Another basic question concerned what, precisely, I was going to study. In other words, what counts as informal teaching and learning? If we pay close attention to the myriad ways in which people learn, through direct teaching as well as through quiet observation, we find that opportunities for learning abound in everyday life. How, then, can a study of informal teaching and learning be contained? Leichter (1979), attempting to place some parameters on the location of education in families and communities, wisely pointed out that some form of selection must take place so that one can "avoid the boundless study of all life" (p. 3).

One issue of definition is whether the term *teaching* necessarily includes learning. Some would argue that if the student has not learned, then the teacher has not taught. This results in an awkward distinction between

---

[7]See Appendix A. The counting process used in generating these percentages can only give a very crude picture of variation. It fails, for example, to differentiate between episodes that went on for 45 minutes or more, and those that lasted only 20 seconds. Thus, the percentages are not to be taken as a set of precise measurements, but rather as a rough estimate of the relative proportions of one type to another.

attempts to teach and actual teaching, in which the instruction may be exactly the same. Should one be called teaching and the other not? I chose, in theory at least, to categorize both as teaching, keeping in mind, however, that the effect on the learner would vary. In actual practice, such situations did not occur because every teaching episode was unique in some way. One can also ask whether one can learn without being taught. Many episodes that I recorded during fieldwork indicate that this is possible. Overt teaching is not needed for learning to take place; in fact, a great deal of learning occurs through observation alone, particularly in the informal realm. My Greek informants were clearly aware of this, for whenever I asked them directly how they had learned a particular skill, they inevitably replied, "I watched" (évlepa).

An interesting example of learning without teaching occured when 4-year-old Alexis became conscious of the red light on my tape recorder. He was amazed to notice that it responded to his voice, and with a wonderfully curious sense of discovery, he began experimenting to determine how it functioned. After asking "How does the little light go on?" (Pos anavei to fotaki;) and "Why does the little light go on?" (Yiati anavei to fotaki;) and receiving only my vague reply, "from your voice" (ap'ti foni sou), he proceeded to test out various consonant and vowel clusters. He found that the light flickered on and off when he uttered a series of plosives, such as "pa pa pa pa" but not when he sustained vowel sounds (e.g., "aaaaa"). After much experimentation, he announced with delight, "It speaks its own language!" (Milaei me ti dhiki tou glossa!).[8]

Although the cognitive activity of learning is invisible, the cues that are available to learners in social interaction are also available to the observer (Shultz & Theophano, 1985). Moreover, learners in interaction sometimes provide overt evidence that they have learned something, called *proximal indicators* of learning. Proximal indicators of learning (such as Alexis' realization that the tape recorder "speaks its own language") occur within or immediately after a teaching and learning episode.[9] Distal indicators, on the other hand, occur over time in subsequent encounters with the same content. Because this was a naturalistic study, I was seldom able to observe repeated occasions of instruction in the same content, so distal indicators of learning were rare. Proximal indicators within teaching and learning

---

[8]This discovery and learning process also illustrates Vygotsky's point that all cognition is social in origin. Other people do not have to be present for learning to be social. In this case, Alexis' learning is mediated in two ways: First, the questions "how" and "why" that he has internalized and used to advantage here mediate his own learning; second, the tape recorder itself, although inhuman, functions in a way as a dialogic "other" that responds to his experiments.

[9]Vygotsky (1978) referred to "microgenetic" analysis in much the same way, as the study of how a psychological process develops in an individual during a single encounter.

episodes occurred frequently however. In the discussions of specific episodes in later chapters, these indicators are noted as they occur. My attention to learning, then, was restricted to observable acts of teaching and learning, or as Wolcott (1982) said, "to those things in the vast repertoire of stuff we carry around in our heads that we have consciously tried to make sense of, or that someone has either succeeded in teaching us or has tried unsuccessfully to teach (thus accounting for things 'not learned')" (p. 101).

Rather than trying to determine through tests or other elicitations whether something has been learned, I have developed "thick descriptions" of informal teaching and learning interactions (Geertz, 1973). I examined these closely to determine the initiation process, the way the roles of teacher and learner are carried out, the way the task or topic is structured, and the relationship between the teaching and the level of the learner. What unifies all the situations I analyze is that there are, at the least, an overtly expressed intent to teach and a common focus on the part of both teacher and learner. Furthermore, although I recorded a number of stories with morals and other monologic speech activities that may be considered a form of teaching, most of the episodes I analyzed involve active participation, either physical or verbal, on the part of *both* a learner and a teacher.

A cultural note about teaching and learning is in order here. In Greek, the verb *mathaino* means both to teach and to learn, with only syntactic marking to show which aspect of the process is meant. English, on the other hand, uses two quite different words. If one takes a Whorfian view,[10] one might argue that this difference shapes the way we think about teaching and learning, encouraging English speakers to conceive of the processes as more separate. Whether or not one accepts the strong linguistic determinism of Whorf's argument, recent work by anthropologists and sociolinguists in non-Western cultures is making it clear that the strong polarity of psychological and social is a construct of our Western culture. In non-mainstream subcultures in the United States, as well as in many other societies, "cultural members hold relatively few such dichotomous views of teaching/teacher and learning/learner" (Heath, 1989, p. 341).

The unit of analysis in this study, then, is the informal teaching and learning episode. I defined this as *a unit of social interaction in which one item, or several items falling under the same topic or task, are overtly taught and/or learned in an particular instance in everyday life outside of school.* Because I wanted to understand the range of informal teaching and learning in the community, I looked across age groups and subject matters.

---

[10]Edward Sapir (1949) argued that the forms of language "predetermine for us certain modes of observation and interpretation" (p. 7). Benjamin Whorf (1956) carried this hypothesis to another level, claiming that because languages differ drastically, the world is experienced differently by speakers of different languages.

I chose the term *episode* over several alternative terms[11] because it seemed the best adapted to the features of informal teaching and learning. It has been used as a unit of discourse analysis, particularly with reference to written text, where paragraphs are often the corresponding surface manifestations of episodes (Van Dijk, 1982). The notion of an episode is especially appropriate for this study because it is a term used in everyday discourse as well as in theoretical discussions; we refer to an episode at a party, for example. Furthermore, it connotes that the unit is a part of a whole, not a whole by itself. This is an important point for informal teaching and learning because they rarely constitute the primary goal of an activity. Rather, moments of instruction tend to occur within an ongoing activity or topic. Sometimes, in fact, teaching and learning can be sprinkled throughout an activity or interspersed among bits of conversation on other topics. The "pieces" of teaching and learning nonetheless revolve around one topic or task, returning again and again like bits of colored thread woven into the fabric of the conversation. I have analyzed these as one episode, not as many.

Informal teaching and learning can best be described as a "fuzzy set" in much the same way that prototypical examples of "birds" have been described. A robin, for example, is considered more prototypical than a chicken or an ostrich (Werner, 1985). Prototypical teaching and learning episodes are those that are easily recognized, by informants as well as by the researcher, as a form of instruction, and the features that make them prototypical can be inferred through analysis and through interviews with the informants. This set of features appears in Appendix B as a model of what constitutes prototypical informal teaching and learning. The five key elements are:

1. an initiation that establishes shared focus,
2. maintenance of shared central focus,

---

[11]The term *speech event* connotes strong boundaries such as those that frame a public lecture (Hymes, 1964, 1972), but informal teaching and learning do not share such strong boundaries. Gumperz' (1982) use of the term *activity* comes closer in terms of its less overt bounding; however it connotes a larger context in which teaching and learning may occur, but which is not constituted by teaching and learning. For example, teaching and learning may occur as a brief sequence *within* the activity of chatting about the weather. The notion of speech act (Searle, 1976), although it is useful at a lower level in analyzing teaching and learning, is too narrow as a basic unit of analysis. Certain speech acts, particularly directives, occur frequently within informal teaching and learning, but in themselves are not enough to constitute informal teaching and learning. For example, a passenger may say to a driver, "Unlock the steering wheel" but this does not mean informal teaching and learning is occurring; it may be simply a reminder to a driver unfamiliar with that car. Finally, all of these terms have a strong linguistic origin; they focus on speech communication. Informal teaching and learning episodes, on the other hand, often have parallel strands of verbal and nonverbal activity.

3. an expert's intent to teach,
4. a novice's intent to learn, and
5. an evaluation.

The most prototypical episodes have all these features. The doorbell episode, for example, is initiated by Alexis as he runs up the front steps exclaiming "the doorbell!" (*to koudhouni*). Throughout the episode, the focus is maintained through dialogue that focuses on the bell, as well as through the posture and gaze direction of the two participants. Grigoris indicates his intent to teach when he says "They don't ring here . . . here, like this" (*Dhen patane edho . . . edho, etsi*) and models the correct way. Alexis indicates his intent to learn when he imitates his grandfather both gesturally (by ringing the bell in the same way) and verbally (by repeating the grandfather's instructions to himself). The evaluation comes in the form of his success in summoning his grandmother from inside and is punctuated by his verbal expressions of delight, a form of self-evaluation.

Not all informal teaching and learning are as prototypical as this episode is. On the other end of the continuum are activities that are part of the everyday stream of life but have few if any of the features listed here. The episodes that I analyzed in depth for this study, however, were all prototypical.

TYPES OF ACTIVITY

A further problem in studying informal teaching and learning across tasks or content areas is that the possible tasks are so many and varied that it becomes difficult to generalize across tasks. In the Greek community where I resided, for example, learning how to dance, how to speak appropriately and politely, and how to make sense of the different kinship terms are very different kinds of learning activities, although they share certain features common to all learning. Perhaps because of the difficulty in comparing across tasks, most researchers who look at informal teaching and learning single out a particular task or class of tasks on which to focus. These include, for example, apprenticeships in tailoring (Lave, 1982), skiing (Burton, Brown & Fischer, 1984), boardsailing compared to surfing and skiing (Miller & Hutchins, 1982), navigation (Gladwin, 1970), family dinners (Shultz & Theophano, 1985), and mathematical problem solving in everyday life (Lave, 1988). Numerous other researchers examine acquisition of and socialization in literacy and language (e.g., Heath, 1983; Ochs, 1982; Schieffelin, 1979; Scollon & Scollon, 1981). Although studies of learning that look across tasks are rare, Greenfield (1984) did compare apprenticeship in weaving in Guatemala with first language acquisition in Los

Angeles. She noted many similarities with regard to the experts' use of scaffolding in the two task environments. As for differences, she found that learners experienced more failure in the language learning situation than in the weaving apprenticeship, perhaps because weaving placed stronger economic constraints on how much the learners could experiment.

In order to make sense of the variety of learning tasks I encountered in the Greek context, I found it necessary to develop a typology of tasks. Typologies in the social sciences are often determined "etically"; that is, a set of categories are derived from earlier work and imposed upon the new data. This can be problematic because the new data may not fit the categories, and important information or insights may as a result be overlooked. In anthropology, on the other hand, fieldworkers are urged to avoid etic categories and to allow the data itself to "suggest" emerging or "emic" categories.[12] Often these emic categories are drawn from the typologies of the informants themselves, thus enhancing, although not guaranteeing, validity. In actual practice, however, much current ethnographic work in the area of cognition uses a combination of emic and etic analyses. I for one found it helpful to know how other researchers had categorized the tasks I was examining, but ultimately the categories I used were the ones that made the most sense in light of my data.

Although it makes intuitive sense to distinguish the different kinds of things we learn, we vary in the ways we draw the lines. Distinctions have been made between "learning about" and "learning to" (Carroll, 1968; Ryle, 1963); among technic, morality, and intellect (Wallace, 1961); and between procedural and declarative (Miller & Hutchins, 1982). These distinctions have been criticized for reflecting "more about the mind-body duality in our own western cultural model of the person than . . . about how cultural knowledge is really organized" (Quinn & Holland, 1987, pp. 8–9). Yet the data I gathered in Greece show that the procedural-declarative distinction does provide a useful and realistic way to make sense of some of the differences among teaching and learning processes. Miller and Hutchins (1982) described the difference as follows:

> Knowing that through traffic has the right of way over vehicles making left turns in an intersection is declarative knowledge. Knowing that there is just enough time for one to safely make the turn before the next approaching car enters the intersection is procedural knowledge. (p. 19)

---

[12]Because "data" is an inanimate subject, it cannot really suggest anything. Statements of this type tend to obscure the fact that it is still the researcher who is responsible for selecting categories of analysis, much as we might prefer to think that our processes of selection are less subjective. See Marshall and Barritt (1990) for an interesting discussion of the language of educational research.

Declarative knowledge, they claimed, is often delivered by verbal instruc-tion, whereas procedural know-how may be "descriptively impenetrable" that is, experts find it difficult if not impossible to teach or explain in words. This point of view, however, is challenged by Gardner (1985), who stated that the six intelligences he has defined[13] can be thought of as " 'sets of know-how'—procedures for doing things." He claimed that "proposi-tional [i.e. declarative] knowledge about intelligences seems to be a particular option followed in some cultures, while of little or no interest in many others" (pp. 68-69). Thus, the verbal–nonverbal distinction may be more productive in comparing culturally patterned modes of learning than in describing procedural and declarative knowledge. For example, many would say that dancing instruction is inherently procedural, and that language instruction is inherently declarative. Yet while dancing is itself a physical process, its instruction need not be procedural; one can learn declaratively that one should not step on the toes of one's partner, and that the fandango is a type of flamenco dance. As for language instruction, it need not be declarative; when one learns how to form the conditional tense in classroom French, one learns first to strip the verb down to its root form, then add the infinitive, and then add the conditional ending. That is certainly a "procedure," although it may be taught declaratively.

In addition to the procedural/declarative distinction, I discerned a third type of teaching and learning in this study. I call it *discrete point* teaching and learning, a term borrowed from the field of second language teaching. In the following citation, it is contrasted to *integrative* teaching: "While 'discrete-point' teaching tries to get students to synthesize a whole language system out of thousands of isolated bits and pieces presented one at a time, 'integrative' teaching presents holistic communicative events and allows students to resolve them analytically into usable elements" (Oller & Oller, 1983, pp. 21-22).[14] Although the distinction referred to here is intended to apply mainly to formal instruction in a second or foreign language, it was useful in understanding some of the informal teaching and learning episodes I encountered, particularly those dealing with communication in the first language.

In order to develop a typology that reflects practice (rather than idealized notions of expected content), we need to know more about which aspect of the subject is being taught, and more importantly, *how* it is being taught. Rather than asking whether a particular content or type of knowledge is

---

[13]Gardner's six intelligences are: linguistic, musical, logicomathematical, spatial, bodily kinesthetic, and personal.

[14]The literature in second language pedagogy looks askance at discrete-point teaching because it creates "another set of isolated bits and pieces of language cut loose from their moorings in experience" (Oller & Oller, 1983, p. 22).

procedural or declarative, we should ask what it means to teach something procedurally or declaratively.

I found that certain features of instruction reveal whether the participants conceive of the activity as a process or as a set of knowledge. These features are the presence and type of modeling, the way the teacher or expert talks, and the organization of the task.

An absence of modeling, for instance, suggests that whatever is being taught is not being taught as a process that could potentially be imitated. If modeling does take place, then it is important to determine the extent to which it is verbal or physical modeling. Procedures, although they can be taught verbally, are most often taught through some sort of iconic modeling in combination with verbal directives. Declarative knowledge, on the other hand, is most often communicated verbally with no modeling (Miller & Hutchins, 1982).

The way a teacher talks reveals several things. First, the verbs that the teacher uses in directives can indicate whether the learner is expected to perform an action (e.g., "move this over here") or absorb a set of propositions (e.g., "remember that . . ."). Action verbs contained in directives indicate that the learner is expected to do something. Verbs that denote states of being or mental processes suggest that the learner is supposed to absorb ideas and propositions rather than perform actions. Second, the teacher's use of deictic expressions[15] tells us the extent to which the referents are present versus "in the head." Procedural teaching usually involves short directives containing an action verb and one or more deictic expressions. The directive refers to a physical action that is being or has been modeled by the teacher. Thus, this form of teacher talk tends to be rather repetitive and restricted, comprising many utterances such as "Do like this" or "Put it again." Declarative teaching involves much more elaborate teacher talk, with explanations and descriptions of objects not present. Deixis is used far less because the subject matter is not a process and not immediate.

Teachers in both formal and informal situations organize subject matter in different ways. Organization can be based on chronology (e.g., do this, then do that, then do the other) in which the teacher creates a narrative to reconstruct an idealized sequence of actions. In this form of organization a process is decomposed into parts or sections, be they interchangeable or in a fixed order. Another type of organization is similar to the expository structure taught to high school and college students in composition courses in the United States. When teachers organize informal learning like

---

[15]Deictic expressions (from the Greek verb, *dheihno,* meaning to show) are those that "require contextual information for their interpretation" (Brown & Yule, 1983), such as *here, now, I, you, this,* and *that.*

TABLE 1
Three Types of Teaching

Procedural	Declarative	Discrete-Point
Physical modeling before or during teaching	No modeling	Verbal modeling before, during, or after teaching
Teacher talk mainly imperative or action verbs and deictics	Teacher talk has more stative verbs, more description, fewer deictics	Teacher talk mainly imperative action verbs but few deictics
Process is decomposed	Focus on elements of a knowledge system	Focus on a single item rather than a process or system

expository prose, they may provide contextualization of the subject matter, for example by giving reasons for learning it or clarifying the consequences of not learning it. In declarative teaching, expository organization is used to present a system of knowledge, and the relationships within that system are pointed out. A third type of instructional organization does not present the subject matter as a chronological sequence or as a logical set of relationships. Rather, it presents isolated bits, usually in the form of a brief correction in the middle of a conversation or activity. This is what distinguishes "discrete-point" teaching from procedural and declarative. It is very likely that these discrete points are part of a bigger system, either procedural or declarative; however they are not overtly treated as such in the interaction.

Characteristics of the three types of teaching are summarized in Table 1. In the chapters that follow, teaching and learning episodes of all three types are examined.

THE PROCESS OF MEDIATION

I now turn to the question of how best to describe the process of teaching and learning. Whether in school or outside of it, teaching and learning involve mediation, a process through which external phenomena are transformed in a learner's mind. In the cases I look at, a teacher or expert plays a key role in helping the learner internalize information from the outside. The expert's role can take many forms, including overt instruction, post-facto correction of errors, modeling, providing guidance at difficult points in the process of task completion, asking questions of the learner that will elicit prior knowledge or focus the learner's attention on a particular aspect of the task, and providing tools or materials to facilitate task completion. The intention is that the task becomes easier or more accessible to the learner. Mediation does not, however, have to be initiated by an expert. Learners can engage others (both intentionally and unintentionally) in mediating roles by asking questions, expressing ignorance or doubt, making errors, or suggesting that both engage in an activity that challenges the learner.

Soviet psychology provides a valuable theoretical framework within which to view informal teaching and learning. Known as the theory of activity, it draws on the work of philosophers and psychologists such as Marx, Engels, Rubinshtein, Bernshtein, and Vygotsky, and is the most comprehensive effort to develop a psychology that links social interaction with individual cognitive development. The Soviet psychologists, whose main articulator is A.N. Leont'ev, propose as a middle link "the subject's activity and its corresponding conditions, goals, and means" (Leont'ev, 1979, p. 46). In other words, by studying learners involved in activity (with other people or with objects), we can view the processes through which external (or social) phenomena are internalized.

Activities, according to Leont'ev, comprise three levels: the activity, which carries with it a motivation; one or more actions that can be taken to realize the activity; and operations, which are the specific nuts and bolts of what one must do to accomplish the actions. Operations are automatic and as such do not require the conscious attention of the learner. Actions, however, must be attended to. When an action has been learned well enough, it drops down to the level of operation and no longer needs conscious attention. This can be visualized easily if one thinks of learning to drive a car with manual transmission. At first, during the process of early learning, one has to attend carefully to shifting, remembering to press down on the clutch with one's foot and to keep it down while moving the gear shift by hand to the proper gear position. Later, after much practice, this action becomes automatic and no longer requires conscious thought. At this point, it has dropped theoretically to the level of an operation. This schema is particularly useful in modeling the process of teaching a physical activity such as ringing a doorbell. Figure 2 shows how these levels might be conceived.

A model such as this can be useful in depicting just which aspects of an activity are being consciously taught and attended to at the level of action. The rendition shown here, based on videotaped interaction, shows that Alexis and Grigoris were attending to very minute aspects of the overall task. If we saw Alexis ringing the doorbell at a later time, we might find that he no longer attended consciously to the processes of reaching the bell and making it ring. Then we could say that those subcomponents had dropped down to the level of operations performed automatically. Although the model helps in understanding the different levels involved in teaching and learning a physical task, it is less helpful in depicting teaching and learning that is not about physical processes. Reasons for this partial applicability are discussed in chapter 6.

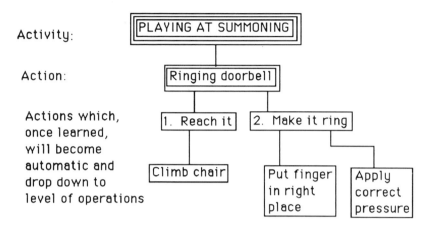

Figure 2.   Levels of activity in ringing the doorbell.

Providing a model to look at task structure is one way the theory of activity has been useful. Another way it informs this study is by emphasizing the ways in which social and cultural contexts mediate learning. Vygotsky's (1978) statement to this effect has been much quoted, but it retains its relevance:

> Any function in the child's cultural development appears twice, or on two planes. First it appears on the social plane, and then on the psychological plane. First it appears between people as an interpsychological category, and then within the child as an intrapsychological category. (p. 57)

To make this theoretical concept more concrete, let us return to Alexis' interaction with Grigoris in ringing the doorbell, for this illustrates quite well the interpenetration of social and psychological that Vygotsky and others refer to. As he attempts to reach and ring the doorbell, Alexis imitates his grandfather both verbally and nonverbally. When the grandfather says "Get up here" Alexis repeats softly (as if the speech were directed in rather than out) "I get up here." When the grandfather says "You'll ring a lot though," Alexis repeats again quietly to himself, "I ring a lot." What we see and hear in the doorbell scene is what Vygotsky referred to as the "transformation between inter- and intra-psychological," as Alexis alters and then appropriates the words of his grandfather for himself. The grandfather's utterances permeate very clearly the utterances of the child.[16]

---

[16] This point is made on a much broader scale by Bakhtin (1986), who stated that "any utterance, when it is studied in greater depth and under the concrete conditions of speech communication, reveals to us many half-concealed or completely concealed words of others with varying degrees of foreignness" (p. 93).

Through the grandfather's help and Alexis' own transformations of this help, Alexis is able to complete the task, to do what he was not initially able to do on his own.

Believing that the best indicator of a learner's development is what he or she can accomplish *with help,* Vygotsky disagreed with Piaget's view of cognitive development as a series of individual, innately determined levels. Vygotsky (1962) posited a "zone of proximal development" which was the distance between the actual and potential level of development.

One kind of social interaction that has received considerable scholarly attention, particularly with regard to the "zone of proximal development," is the dialogue that typically goes on between mainstream American mothers and children. The term *scaffolding* has been used to refer metaphorically to the help the mother gives on her side of the dyad:

> She reduces the degrees of freedom with which the child has to cope, concentrates his attention into a manageable domain, and provides models of the expected dialogue from which he can extract selectively what he needs for filling his role in discourse. . . . [She also extends] the situations in which and the functions for which different utterances or vocalizations can be used. . . . Finally, the mother plays the role of communicative ratchet: once the child has made a step forward, she will not let him slide back. (Bruner, 1978, p. 254)

Although Bruner and his colleagues did not originally work within the Soviet paradigm described earlier, their work is for the most part mutually compatible in that the notion of scaffolded dialogue elaborates on one of the ways mothers work within the child's zone of proximal development. Many other researchers have taken up the scaffolding metaphor, extending it to tasks other than first language acquisition, and to the formal environment of school rather than dialogue at mother's side.

Similar to scaffolding is another process called *shaping.* This term was originally used by Skinner (1938) to refer to the process through which a learner, by successive reinforcements, moves from innaccurate to accurate performance of a task. Greenfield (1984) reinterpreted the original meaning as follows:

> Both [scaffolding and shaping] create an environment which reduces both error and failure experiences at the early stages of learning a new skill. There is, however, a major difference between them. Shaping involves a series of successive approximations to the ultimate task goal. While the learner is successful at every point in the process, he or she starts with a simplified version of the ultimate task. Scaffolding, in contrast, does not involve simplifying the task during the period of learning. Instead, it holds the task constant while simplifying the learner's role through the graduated intervention of the teacher. (p. 119)

According to Greenfield, both scaffolding and shaping are instrumental in learning. Whether the task is held constant and the learner's role in it simplified, or whether the task is simplified to allow for full learner participation, in either case the learner has an opportunity to experience mastery. Sometimes mastery is evident in the activity itself, and other times it appears in subsequent encounters with the same or a similar task. In the doorbell episode, we saw a form of scaffolding in which the task (ringing the doorbell) remained constant, but the teacher, Grigoris, intervened to enable Alexis to complete the task.

FRAMING

Even in the most congruous educational encounters, participants can have different frames of reference. A teacher or expert, for example, can view an interaction as a friendly talk, whereas a child can view the same interaction as a test of some sort. A study of informal teaching and learning must incorporate some way of describing and accounting for these frames of reference, for if instruction is to be successful, participants must share understanding not only of the goal of the activity, but also of the interpretive framework within which it is carried out.

The notion of *frame* was introduced by Bateson (1972), who pointed out that monkeys, as well as human beings and other animals, seem to know quite well when an apparently threatening gesture is to be taken as play-at-combat rather than combat. Bateson suggested that a metacommunicative signalling system allows us to cue one another as to the interpretive frame within which our actions can be understood. In the doorbell scene, it is clear to all the participants that Alexis is playing, and that the ringing of the bell does not constitute a true "summons" to Katerina to open the door. Although she does in fact open it, she does so to participate in the game and to humor Alexis.

When an individual recognizes and understands a particular event, he or she responds in terms of a "primary framework." In the doorbell scene, the primary framework would be truly ringing a doorbell to summon someone to the door. The primary framework renders "what would otherwise be a meaningless aspect of the scene into something that is meaningful" (Goffman, 1974, p. 21). It does so without recourse to another, more fundamental framework on which this one is based. However, that same activity can be transformed, through a process Goffman called "keying," to mean something different from its meaning in the primary framework. The doorbell ringing scene is keyed to become play rather than the real thing.

Keying can be illustrated as well by a situation in which two children appear to be fighting. If indeed they are fighting, and both understand their behavior as fighting, then this can be called a primary framework. If, on the other hand, they are really only playing, then we can say that the primary framework (fighting) has undergone a process of transformation (keying) that gives it a different meaning than it would have had in its primary interpretive frame. Normally the primary frame goes unmarked, and "response in frame terms is unlikely unless doubt needs combating, as in the reply, 'No, they're not merely playing; it's a real fight'" (Goffman, 1974, p. 46).

The notion of framing is related to kidding and teasing as well as to play. When an adult teases a child, he or she transforms a primary activity to something else. The child, however, may continue to believe that the activity is the primary, or "real" one, and thus be "contained" in a frame over which the adult has control. In other words, there are frames in which all participants mutually agree, "This is play" and there are frames in which one or more participants are unaware that a transformation is in effect. These Goffman called "fabrications," of which kidding and teasing are one manifestation.

In some societies, "extensive teasing marks early talk to children," and thus "they must attend first to signals that mark or frame these utterances as play and only secondarily to referential content" (Heath, 1989, p. 339). In Greece, as noted in Friedls' ethnography of the village called Vasilika, teasing receives considerable emphasis. However, like culture, frames are not static. People in interaction are constantly revising and elaborating their frames of expectation in accordance with what is happening at the moment (Erickson, 1982; Gumperz, 1982). It is particularly important, then, to consider how framing is manifested in the informal teaching and learning explored in this study.

2 The Communities

TRIKALA AND KIRIAKITSA

The Central Greek province of Thessaly, where this study was conducted, consists largely of flat, fertile plains. Considered the "breadbasket" of Greece, Thessaly grows most of the wheat the country uses, as well as corn, cotton, watermelons, and many other crops. It has several medium-sized cities, one of which is Trikala.

A city of approximately 30,000 inhabitants and the seat of the local prefecture, Trikala is about 5 hours north of Athens by car or bus. To the north lie the sandstone promontories of Meteora, which are well known for the 13th-century Byzantine monasteries perched on top of the cliffs. To the west are the Pindus mountains, whose outlines are usually hazy from smoke and dust. To the east across the plains lies a larger city, Larissa, and to the south is the small city of Karditsa (see Figure 3 for map).

Tourists pass through Trikala on their way to the magnificent formations at Meteora, but they rarely stay. The historical sites in Trikala do not cater to tourism, and unless one is interested in the everyday life of a fairly typical Greek town with a river (the Lithaios) and a fort built in the middle ages, there is little for tourists to do there. For this reason, Trikala is a far cry from the Greek islands most outsiders think of when they picture Greece.

Kiriakitsa, a large village of approximately 1,800 inhabitants or 300 houses,[1] is located four kilometers from Trikala. In fact, Kiriakitsa is so close to Trikala that it is considered a suburb or *sinikeia* within the city

---

[1] Population estimate from the Dimarheia (town hall) in Trikala, June 1986.

Figure 3. Map of the area near Trikala (from the American Automobile Association, Heathrow, FL 32746. 1991–92 edition).

limits and jurisdiction, even while maintaining its separate village characteristics.[2]

To reach the village of Kiriakitsa from Trikala, one travels on a paved road past fields of wheat, watermelons, and corn in the summer months; cotton, sugarbeets and cabbage in the fall and winter. Traffic is generally light; one passes a few tractors, bicycles, horse-drawn carts, motorbikes, cars, and an occasional pedestrian. To the right as one approaches Kiriakitsa, the Pindus mountains loom out of the haze. In all other directions the land is flat and cultivated, with poplar, fig, and walnut trees lined in bunches along roadsides or at the edges of fields. The earth is dark,

[2]The fact that Kiriakitsa is relatively large, accessible, and close to a major city makes it different from the Greek villages examined in earlier ethnographies (e.g., DuBoulay, 1974; Friedl, 1962; Herzfeld, 1980; McNall, 1974), which focus on places that represent traditional and/or dying ways of life. Cowan (1990), in her recent ethnography of dance in a northern Greek town, commented similarly on the lack of attention to new and evolving forms of Greek culture.

fertile, and far moister than in other areas of Greece due to considerable rainfall and a high water table.

Before reaching the first village houses, one passes a *taverna* (restaurant and entertainment center) on the right, a small white church, *Agios Giorgios,* in a park on the left, then the village cemetary and the weighing station also on the left. The village houses are mostly one-story, white or light-colored stucco, with reddish tile roofs. Next to the recent buildings stand earlier ones of adobe brick and other construction, often serving as stables, chicken houses, or tool sheds. Villagers prefer to use an old building for something else rather than to tear it down. Most houses have a front porch or *avli* facing East,[3] where women sit in the warmer months to shell peas, braid garlic, peel potatoes, and do other sedentary work. The smell of woodsmoke usually hangs in the air as a good deal of the cooking is still done in woodburning ovens either indoors or outdoors. Weeds and other plant materials are also frequently burned to clear the fields.

The road passes the first few houses and then turns left into the village square, where it circles around the fountain and the plane tree that stand in the flagstone area at the center (Figure 4). Around the center are all the stores and community buildings: the Church of St. Charalambos (patron saint of Kiriakitsa); the elementary school (Grades 1–6); the kindergarten; two cafeneia where wine, beer, *cipporo,*[4] soft drinks, and appetizers are served; a small market; a butcher's shop; and a kiosk that sells candy, cigarettes, newspapers, bandaids, and aspirin.

Kiriakitsa is peopled by three ethnic groups: Karagounides,[5] Vlachs, and Gypsies or *Tsingani.* These groups have lived near one another for centuries, maintaining separate domains that allow for relatively peaceful co-existence in spite of the rather marked differences between them. The differences that I outline now exist not only at the village level, but also at the levels of city and region. Although I did not specifically study ethnic groups other than the Karagounides, it is nonetheless important to frame the smaller differences I found among neighbors and family members in the context of the ethnic groups that constitute the larger social structure.

The Karagounides, by far the largest and most established of the three groups, are Greek-speaking farmers who own most of the houses and land in Kiriakitsa. They are allegedly descended from ancient Greek tribes who settled the plains of Thessaly as early as the fourth century B.C. The Vlachs, traditionally a nomadic group who speak a Latin-based language called

---

[3]East is the direction of the rising sun and of Constantinople, former center of Greek Orthodoxy. The dead are buried facing East as well.

[4]*Cipporo* is a locally produced spirit made from grapes, very similar in taste to ouzo, the anise flavored drink that is sold commercially.

[5]Karagounides is the plural form of the singular Karagounis (m.) or Karagouna (f.).

Figure 4. Central square in Kiriakitsa (photo by Panos Panagos, 1991).

Vlachica, appeared in the area around the tenth century A.D. and lived primarily in the foothills and mountains of the Pindus range (Papadimou, 1980). At the time of the study, they had begun buying land and building houses on the outskirts of Kiriakitsa. The Gypsies around Kiriakitsa are semi-nomadic; many own houses outside of Trikala and Karditsa (the next town to the south), but during the summer months they set up tent communities close to the watermelon fields and buy truckloads of watermelons from the Karagounides, which they then sell all over Greece (see Figure 5). During my stay in Kiriakitsa, a community of Gypsies lived in a field on the southern edge of the village from June until August, the height of watermelon season. During the rest of the year, Gypsies frequently passed through the village in trucks with megaphones, announcing produce, furniture, rugs, and blankets for sale.

As for the relationship among the three groups, I can only comment as an outsider who is familiar with the Karagounides' point of view. The Vlachs and the Gypsies surely have other stories to tell. That there is negative stereotyping among all three is certain, and because the Karagounides are the majority and the dominant group, their negative stereotyping of Vlachs and Gypsies results in social disadvantages for these groups.

However, the Vlachs, because they are as a group economically successful, occupy a much higher rung on the social ladder than the Gypsies. When I questioned Karagounides about the reason for the Vlachs' success in business, I was told that during the four centuries of Turkish occupation, the nomadic Vlachs avoided being subjugated to the Turks, whereas the settled, agrarian Karagounides became serfs and slaves. The Vlachs were thus able to develop their culture and to educate their children in relative freedom; this freedom is cited as the reason that until recently, more Vlachs than Karagounides became successful businessmen and professionals. It is now acceptable, although still noteworthy, for Karagounides to intermarry with Vlachs. The Karagounides continue to hold negative stereotypes of the Vlachs, but they are mild ones having to do with perceived aggression and clannishness.

Karagounides do not consider it at all acceptable, however, to intermarry with Gypsies. Villagers view the Gypsies as a people shrouded in mystery who can cast evil spells and steal before one's very eyes. Gypsies are considered not only untrustworthy, but also dirty, smelly, and badly behaved. In fact, there is a derogatory word for Gypsy, *yiftos,* which is extended metaphorically to designate any person who is dishonest, dirty, or mean. Social contact with the Gypsies is far more restricted than with the Vlachs; where Vlachs and Karagounides associate freely even to the point of intermarriage, Gypsies and Karagounides hardly speak to one another except in commercial interactions such as the selling and buying of watermelons. Children are socialized very early to keep their distance, as I

Figure 5. Two gypsy boys at the watermelon marketplace.

noticed on several occasions when Gypsy children coming into the neighborhood were shunned and regarded with suspicion by the other children.

Residents and outsiders alike agree that in Kiriakitsa there is little village pride. People who have lived or visited in other villages, particularly more isolated ones, cite as an example of this lack of pride that there is no *volta*.[6] They also note that villagers do not make any particular effort at beautifying the small school buildings or the areas around them, for example by cleaning up the field where the children play during recess. Furthermore, major events such as marriages and baptisms are usually celebrated at *kentro's* (entertainment centers) on the highway between Trikala and Kalambaka, rather than on the villagers' property. When, during the course of my stay, a marriage celebration did take place in the village, people noted it as unusual and became quite nostalgic about how things used to be in the old days, when all such events were celebrated in the village.

No matter what people cited as evidence, they all agreed that the one major factor contributing to this lack of village pride is the proximity of Trikala and the increased availability of transportation between village and town. A bus runs between the two seven times a day, and a number of people now have cars. Thus, it is relatively easy to go into Trikala for the evening *volta* as well as for shopping. The shopping and entertainment that is available in town is considered better than any the village could offer. This was illustrated clearly by the case of the butcher's shop that a villager's son (the same one who celebrated his marriage in the village) opened recently in the central square. The family I lived with made a point of buying meat there frequently because they wanted to support the butcher's effort and appreciated the quality of the meat he sold. However, very few villagers felt this way; the majority preferred to buy their meat in town even if it meant an extra trip, simply because they felt a villager's product to be qualitatively and socially inferior. Thus, it was questionable whether the butcher would be able to stay in business.

FAMILY AND NEIGHBORHOOD

The Family

Figure 6 shows the structure of the family with whom I spent the majority of my time. Grigoris Yorgakis was born in the village of Kiriakitsa in 1914.

---

[6]The *volta* is a kind of promenade common in Mediterranean countries in which well-dressed couples and families stroll up and down the main street chatting, looking at shop windows, and stopping for a drink or snack at a sidewalk cafe where one can view passers-by. The street is closed to vehicles during the *volta* (3 or 4 hours every evening) and foot traffic moves in a very orderly fashion using the right side of the street to go up, and the left to come back. If one walks on the wrong side, as I did at first, one is said to be going *anapoda* (in reverse).

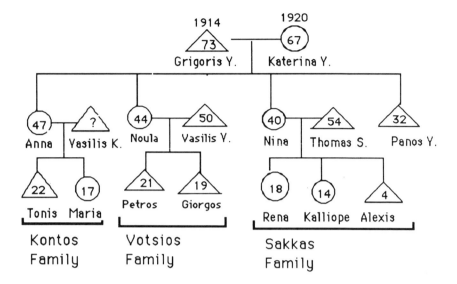

Figure 6.   The Yorgakis Family.

His father was a chorister (*psaltis*), and both his parents made their living as farmers. In 1939, Grigoris married Katerina Karagouni, the 19-year-old daughter of a neighboring farmer. Grigoris and Katerina had four children:

- Anna, born 1939, 47 years old (all ages at the time of the study)
- Noula, born 1942, 44 years old
- Nina, born 1947, 40 years old
- Panos, born 1954, 32 years old

Anna married Vasilis Kontos, an accountant from a nearby village, and they established their home in the town of Trikala, 4 kilometers from Kiriakitsa. Anna runs a beauty shop below their apartment and Vasilis works for the bus company, KTEL. At the time of the study their oldest child, Tonis, was studying business at the university in Thessaloniki, about 3 hours from Trikala. Maria, their youngest, was living with her parents and studying to pass the Panhellenic Exams so that she too could attend university. Tonis spent most of the summer with the family in Trikala, and visited about once a month while school was in session. The family income is considered middle class in Greek society. They own the two-unit building where they live as well as a used Renault (the first car they have owned), which they bought shortly before I began fieldwork. They were also paying for Tonis' housing in Thessaloniki and expected to pay for Maria's as well if she was accepted to the university.

Noula, the second daughter, is also a hairdresser. She lives in Larisa, a larger town than Trikala about 1 hour's drive to the east. Her husband, Vasilis Votsios, was born in a mountain village and is a major in the Greek Army. Because of his career they had moved several times, living during the early years of their marriage on Cyprus, then in Athens, and at the time of the study in Larisa. Their oldest son, Petros, was living at home and studying forestry at a technical college. He was also applying to American universities for further studies in biology. Giorgos, the younger son, was serving his mandatory 2 years in the Greek Army, having tried twice and failed to get into Greek university.[7] The Votsios family is also middle class, but unlike the Kontos family they do not own their own home. They do, however, have a used car and a small vacation home in the village where Vasilis was born. Noula's hairdressing business is operated out of their apartment, with a smaller clientele than Anna's. They were expecting to support Petros' study abroad and to set Giorgos up in some kind of business after he finished his Army service.

The youngest daughter, Nina, is the third and last in the line of hairdressers.[8] She and her husband, Thomas Sakkas, and three children live about two blocks from Anna in Trikala. Thomas, born and raised in Trikala, drives a bus for the local service connecting the town with nearby villages. Rena, their oldest daughter, was living at home, caught at the difficult crossroads where university study was no longer possible (she had tried to pass the exams twice) and other options had not yet crystallized. She was anxious to leave Trikala, but did not have the economic wherewithal to do so without a firm job. Kalliope, the younger of the two daughters, was attending the gymnasium (equivalent to ninth grade in U.S. system). The youngest child, Alexis, was 4 and had not yet attended any school. The Sakkas family owns their own apartment, as well as a car and the bus that Thomas uses in his work. Nina rents the space for her beauty salon a few blocks from their home. Like the other two families, they were expecting to either support their children's higher education or set them up in a business.

Grigoris and Katerina's youngest child and only son, Panos, left Greece in 1977 at the age of 23 to come to the United States. At the time of the study, he was still living in the United States, where he had recently finished

---

[7]All Greek males are required to serve 2 years in the Army; for Tonis and Petros, this service was to be completed after they finish their studies.

[8]It is no accident that all three daughters became hairdressers. The pattern dates back to Katerina's insistence, when Anna was in her late teens, that the girls all "learn a trade" (na mathoun mia techni) so that they could "escape the village" (na ksefigoun ap'to horio). She met resistance from the girls' father, who did not foresee the need for women to have cash income of their own and felt it was unseemly for village girls to work outside the village. However, Katerina prevailed and sent the girls to Trikala to learn. They set up a shop together, and eventually after marrying each developed her own business.

a BFA in Film. He was divorced and had plans to return eventually to Greece to work in film or television there.

The Neighborhood

Grigoris and Katerina, besides sharing strong bonds with their children and grandchildren, also form an integral part of the village neighborhood in which they live. This neighborhood consists of 10 families, almost all of whom are kin of various degrees. I was particularly interested in the neighborhood because I wanted to understand the contexts of informal teaching and learning — who teaches whom, when, why, and where. Because informal teaching and learning depends on face-to-face interaction, it was important to explore the nature of contacts shared among neighborhood members. Looking at the social structure of the neighborhood from a network point of view enabled me to see why informal teaching and learning occurred more between some families than others.

It was not entirely clear right away what constituted the neighborhood. Proximity of course played an important role, but where proximity ended (that is, when a household was "too far" to be part of the neighborhood) varied. Kinship was also important, but like proximity it was not enough in itself to determine the boundaries of a neighborhood. A family could bear the most tenuous kinship to other neighborhood families yet still be part of the neighborhood. Kin could also live beyond the neighborhood but still in the village, as was the case with several of Grigoris' and Katerina's sisters and their families. What, then, constitutes a neighborhood besides the obvious kinship and proximity?

During my 8 months as a participant observer, I had ample opportunity to note the comings and goings of villagers who bore some relation, kin or other, to Grigoris and Katerina. Toward the end of the study I had developed a fairly clear notion of who constituted the neighborhood and why. However, there were some fuzzy edges — people who, according to my interpretation, should belong but did not seem to, and people who should not belong but somehow did. In an interview with Grigoris, I learned more about how he expresses the notion of neighborhood and was able thus to refine my own interpretations.

The interpretation of neighborhood is also based on principals used in network analysis, noted earlier in chapter 1. The neighborhood constituted a "high density" network because the contacts of any one individual all knew each other. Individuals also interacted with one another in more than one capacity (e.g., neighbors were also kin and friends), creating what are called "multiplex role relationships" (Milroy, 1980).

Using these principles, Grigoris' comments and my own observations, I derived a set of relational factors that contributed either singly or in clusters to inclusion in the neighborhood. Appendix C shows the 10 households, their kinship to household 1 and to each other, and the relational factors that apply. In the explanation of these factors that follows, the numbers of the households for whom this was a factor during the period of my stay are listed. In fact, it was often only one *individual* from a household who actively produced the bonding I refer to, but because my informants tended to view individuals as representatives of their households, I too have assumed that in these cases individuals act on behalf of or with the support of their households.

a. Proximity   Houses must be close enough so that frequent visiting is practical. This usually means practical on foot because most villagers do not have cars and most female villagers do not ride bicycles. Proximity is a factor for all households in the neighborhood. Figure 7 shows their arrangement.

b. Kinship   Kinship in the village can be of three types: blood, marriage, or fictive. Fictive kinship is the relationship of best man/woman to bride/groom, and godfather/godmother to child (*koumbaros and nonos*). Villagers value these relationships almost as highly as kinship by blood or marriage. All households share some kinship relation with at least one other household in the neighborhood.

c. Children   Families whose children play together also accept a certain degree of bonding between the adults. If children visit between one

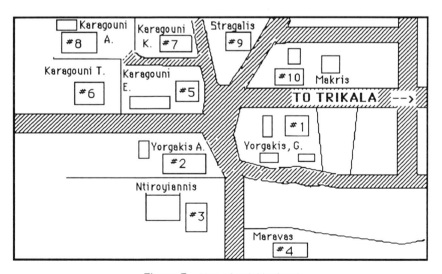

Figure 7. Map of neighborhood.

another's houses, then the adults take on the temporary caretaking role for whatever children are on the property at a given time. Children move quite freely among certain of the neighborhood households, visiting without prior invitation. However, in return for the open door policy the adults retain the right to shoo the children out whenever visiting is inconvenient (Households 1, 2, 3, 4, 5, 6, 8, and 10; Households 7 and 9 have no children).

d. Tools and Equipment Perhaps *because* certain rights and obligations within the network are assumed, families do not own all the tools or equipment they might use. Items that are used only on an occasional or seasonal basis may be shared and borrowed between households, always with the understanding that the item belongs to the household that originally bought it. Some examples of tools and equipment that were shared/borrowed are a pesticide sprayer, a wheat grinding stone, a jack for a car, wheelbarrows (most families have one, but occasionally need to borrow a second), and a hairdryer (Households 1, 2, 3, 5, 6, and 8).

e. Food When certain vegetables or fruits are in season and one household has an abundance of something lacking in another household, a member of the first household may spontaneously bring some of the produce to another. Sometimes this gift is part of a visit that includes some sort of service or tool exchange. A member of a household may also go to another household known to have an abundance of produce and ask specifically to pick or take some. Occasionally these food exchanges involved cooked food made in bulk (such as jams) as well as fresh produce (Households 1, 2, 3, 5, 6, and 8).

f. Services When members of one household are unable to perform a certain task, they may go to another household where someone is known to be able to perform the needed service. Examples include mending a scythe, helping children with homework, and doctoring. However, the doctoring is so frequent and specialized that I have separated it as a special relationship (Households 1, 2, 4, 5, 6, and 8).

g. Doctoring Grigoris and Katerina were frequently called on to measure people's blood pressure and to administer intramuscular injections.[9] When I asked how this state of affairs came about , Grigoris replied "I'm a fake doctor" (*Eimai pseftoyiatros*), and explained that he had learned how

---

[9]Disposable hypodermic needles are sold over the counter in Greece. Doctors prescribe medicine to be taken by injection far more often than they do in the United States, and it is expected that a family member or friend will give the injection as often as it is prescribed.

to perform these basic medical services in the Army years ago; Katerina had then learned from him. Because the injections are usually given in the buttocks, modesty and gender become important; Katerina takes care of the women, Grigoris the men (Households 1, 2, 4, 5, 6, 8, and 10).

h. Unannounced Visiting   Lest the reader think that all contact in the neighborhood involves some sort of service or goods exchange, I want to point out that visiting simply for the sake of visiting is also frequent, although not among all the families. Visitors often do not provide any explicit reason for the visit, but when they do, the reasons may include the following: time to spare while waiting for the bus; the need to get out of the house, which was especially prevalent among young mothers and was often expressed as "I was ready to explode/burst" (*Eiha skasei*) ; and exchange of neighborhood and local news. The latter was *always* a function of the visits, though it was not always overtly expressed as such (Households 1, 2, 3, 4, 5, 6, and 8).

Although all 10 of these households are, by Grigoris and Katerina's definitions, included in the neighborhood, Households 7 and 10 are considered very much outsiders and fulfill very few of the relational functions just listed. Because their marginality directly affects the *amount* of informal teaching and learning that goes on between these families and the rest of the neighborhood, a closer look is warranted.

Households 7 and 10 both bear kinship and proximity relations to Grigoris and Katerina's and most of the other households in the neighborhood, and the children of Household 10 play freely with the other neighborhood children. However, although these factors seem to be sufficient for inclusion in the neighborhood, it is important to note that they do not involve any active relational work on the part of the adults. One can be kin, live close by, and allow one's children to play with other neighborhood children without ever going to another neighborhood house or inviting visitors into one's own. This drastically reduces the number of potential environments where informal teaching and learning can take place. In fact, during the entire 8 months of my stay, no adults from Households 7 or 10 ever visited at Grigoris and Katerina's, nor were we free to drop by. In one rather poignant case, I walked after school with several neighborhood children from the kindergarten back to the neighborhood. When I left 5-year-old Giorgos (of Household 10) at his gate, he wanted me to follow. I said "Not now," and he remarked wistfully, "You never come to visit at our house, but you go to all the other kids' houses." For a period of about a week when the grandmother of Household 10 was ill, Katerina or Grigoris would go to doctor her, but this was the only time when I observed the adults of Household 10 initiating interaction with the neighbors.

That these two households were off limits became clear to me very early in my stay, and was all the more marked by contrast to the more general rule of hospitality. Members of the other households talked with me about the closed door policy of Households 7 and 10, suggesting reasons for their isolation that included bad character, stinginess, unsociability, and in the case of Household 7, bad influence of other family members (e.g., "The man used to be OK, but he married a crazy woman, and his daughter is crazy too, so now he has become like them").

Two other households deserve special mention here because they too are in some senses on the fringe of the neighborhood. Household 4 bears no kin relation to any neighborhood households except Household 10, and is the farthest, in terms of physical distance, and the most isolated of all the neighborhood. The land on which it rests is legally designated as a "field" (*horafi*) rather than a residential lot, and as a result it was only in October 1986 that they finally had enough money to pay the city of Trikala to extend the telephone line. Most houses in the village have had telephone service since the 1970s. On the one hand, not having a telephone increased the isolation of Household 4, but on the other hand it created a dependence on other households in the neighborhood in that members of Household 4 had to visit in order to use the telephone. Another factor that may contribute to their "fringe-like" quality is that Alekos, Agouri's husband, is from the area near Thessaloniki, 3 hours to the northeast, and makes his living as a trucker carrying goods all over northern and central Greece. Thus, he is seldom home, his roots are elsewhere, and he shares little with other men in the neighborhood, most of whom make their living by farming.

During my fieldwork, it was mainly Agouri and her children who would initiate contact with the neighborhood. Agouri would come into the more central area of the neighborhood in order for her children to find playmates, and while the children played, Agouri would visit with anyone present. The contact was asymmetrial, however, for despite Agouri's frequent visits to Grigoris and Katerina's and other households, rarely did anyone visit her at her household. Unlike most of the other neighbors, who frequently asked me to drop by, Agouri never extended an invitation. In this sense, the Maravas household resembled Households 7 and 10, the outsiders; yet it was clear that the neighbors did not consider Agouri and her family to be in the same category. This difference must have been due to Agouri's frequent reaching out with her children to other members of the neighborhood.

The last household I want to mention in this section is Household 9, the home of Nikos Stragalis. Nikos, born in 1903, was 83 years old at the time of the study and lived alone. He was seldom a participant in neighborhood visiting or exchanges of goods and services, yet the central location of his house afforded him a good vantage point from which to view the activities of the neighbors. During the warmer months he would often sit on his front porch and greet people on their way to or from the central square. I personally had little contact with him until one day in November when Grigoris took me to his house to interview him. Apparently delighted with the company and my interest in his life and viewpoints, he then made a point of telephoning frequently, usually to add one more detail to the story of Alexander the Great, whose history he was reading. He also took Grigoris and me to visit his daughter and granddaughter in a nearby village one Sunday. Thus, although Nikos did not appear at first to be a very active producer of network bonds as I have outlined them here, his activity toward the end of my stay convinced me that he is indeed a member of the neighborhood. Grigoris and Katerina confirmed this, adding that he is also Noula's godfather and therefore very much kin.

This was the setting in which I conducted my study. My contacts radiated outward from the Yorgakis family, and were to a large extent determined by *their* social contacts. Thus, I interacted most frequently with immediate family members, both in the village and in Trikala and Larisa, and members of the neighborhood. Most of the informal teaching and learning that I observed took place within the matrix of immediate family and neighborhood. Frequent observations in the neighborhood gave me a comparative perspective on the actions of the central Yorgakis characters. Less frequently, I had contact with other villagers, as for example when we would visit other relatives, be invited to a name day celebration, or attend a marriage, baptism, or funeral. I also met villagers when I went to the village square to get mail or shop at the small grocery store, when I went running in the park near *Agios Georgios,* and when I attended the village kindergarten. My contacts with townspeople in Trikala, unless they were relatives or friends of the family, were limited to interactions in shops, in the town hall where I collected some statistics and maps, in the very small English-speaking community, and in the hospital where Grigoris stayed for several days with bronchitis. I observed little informal teaching and learning in these settings.

The next chapter discusses in greater detail my role in the community and the methods used to collect and analyze data.

3 Fieldwork in Kiriakitsa and Trikala

Ethnographers in the past, although they often established authority by giving brief accounts of how they gained entry to a community, rarely offered readers insight into the ethnographer's role and the particular methodological problems encountered. Currently, however, a shift toward more reflexive ethnographic writing encourages the examination of the place of the narrator/observer (Hess, 1989). This approach, although criticized by some as "self-indulgent" (e.g., Pratt, 1986, p. 31), can provide insight in at least two ways, enabling readers to understand fieldwork as a process rather than a completed effort and allowing them to judge for themselves how the participant observer influenced the data that were gathered. With these objectives in mind, I focus here on central issues surrounding my roles in the community and the methods of data collection.

In the Preface, I described how I gained access to the communities of Kiriakitsa and Trikala. Throughout the 8 months of fieldwork I lived in the village, where I had a room in the Yorgakis house. This household included Katerina, Grigoris, and often Alexis, their 4-year-old grandson, who spent about half his time in the village and half with his parents in Trikala. Other members of the family — Rena, Kalliope, and Petros — also stayed occasionally. Sometimes I would spend 2 or 3 days in Trikala with one of the daughters' families, but there was not enough space in these apartments for me to have a room or work area, so I always returned to the village for writing and analytical work. From the window near my desk, I could look out onto the road and monitor the activities of the neighborhood. Children from all the nearby households, sometimes as many as 10 or 15, would typically gather in the road to play as it was easier for everyone not to have them in backyards or houses unless the weather was bad. Adults passed my window regularly on their way to and from the fields and/or town. Their rhythms became familiar to me—the two shepherds who would drive their sheep past each morning at about 6 a.m., the hooves softly hurrying along the road accompanied by baa-ing and the deep sound of bells; a little later, the neighbors who went out to the fields with horses and empty metal carts bouncing behind; then various people driving tractors, some pulling carts, some not. And in between would be quiet bicyclists and pedestrians. In the early afternoon the process reversed itself as people returned for the midday meal (*mesimerino*). Sometimes the carts would be loaded high then, creaking under the weight of huge sacks of cotton or other crops. Around 5 or 6 p.m., during the months when there was enough light, there would be another exodus to the fields, returning by dusk.

I participated as much as possible in whatever activities the family members, particularly female, engaged in. This included, on an almost daily basis, preparing food, caring for children, working in the fields, and visiting neighbors and relatives. All family members made frequent trips between town and village because two of the daughters and their families lived in town. Less frequently, I participated in special occasions, including visits to or from the Votsios family in Larisa and community events such as religious holidays, marriages, baptisms, and funerals.

Before beginning fieldwork, I had planned to tell the informants that I was studying their everyday life, thinking that this would suffice as an explanation while at the same time not being so specific that they might become self-conscious in their teaching and learning. However, upon arrival I quickly realized that this explanation was too vague; they knew that "everyday life" is too big to study. Rather than lie to them, I told them, in as many ways as I could, what I was really studying. I doubt that they ever completely understood; as Goffman (1974) pointed out, " . . . even when the student informs his subjects that he is engaged in studying them, they are unlikely to appreciate in detail what sorts of facts he is collecting. . . ." (p. 171). It is difficult for a Greek villager to conceive of why his or her informal teaching and learning could possibly be of interest to an American researcher. When people verbalized what they thought I was studying, they spoke of "traditions" (*paradosies*), "folklore" (*laographia*), or "customs" (*ithi kai ethima*). In other words, it made sense to them that I would come to study the practices of bygone eras but not current, everyday modes of teaching and learning, which to them were unremarkable. Cowan (1990) encountered a similar response when she studied Greek dance events in their more modern contexts. Furthermore, the situations in which I was visibly gathering data through recordings were so varied (e.g., mealtime conversation, children at play, adults working together . . .) that informants must have found it difficult to imagine what common thread united these situations. Indeed, at times I wondered too.

Trikala is not a city with heavy tourism, and there is virtually no foreign-born community. My presence was therefore highly unusual, and the opportunity to observe and interact with a foreigner who was not just "passing through" must have influenced people's views of what it means to be from another culture. In the village there were no other foreigners and only one Greek who spoke English fluently. Oddly enough I was not introduced to her until I had been there for 7 months. In Trikala there were three native English-speaking residents, with whom I met only once. I was very much immersed, having little to no interaction with anyone outside the communities of Kiriakitsa, Trikala, and Larisa.

THE ETHNOGRAPHER'S ROLE

My roles in the village community were complex and at times difficult to orchestrate. The most salient and consistent role was that of daughter-in-law (*nifi*). Other roles included that of researcher, older sister, English tutor, and employer (the latter when I hired one of the informants to transcribe tapes). The role of researcher, although very important in my own mind, was not so salient to the informants. They preferred to introduce me to others as their *nifi,* almost never mentioning the research in the first 5 or 10 minutes of conversation.[1] The only times they introduced me as a researcher as well as a *nifi* were when I carried the videocamera, which required some kind of rationale to explain its presence. Outside the village, however, unless I was with a family member, the role of researcher became primary because the people I interacted with were for the most part not kin of the Yorgakis family.

In a discussion of the roles of single women in fieldwork, Golde (1986) noted that techniques are often devised by locals to provide protection or simply to symbolize it, thus reducing either the woman's accessibility or her desirability.

> These include finding a man or men whose roles enable them to serve as protectors; moving in with a family; taking or being assigned an already existing role that minimizes or neutralizes sexuality or is a traditionally protected one, such as "child," "sister," "grandmother"; working chiefly with the women and children of the community or living in the field with a husband or a team of fellow workers. (p. 6)

By casting me primarily as *nifi,* the Yorgakis family and other villagers sidestepped the many difficult and potentially threatening issues that could

---

[1]See Milroy (1980) for a similar account.

have arisen had I not come with the essential family connection. This also made it more comfortable for me to do fieldwork and obviated the need for elaborate explanations of who I was and what I was doing there.

The power of the kinship connection is illustrated in a formulaic question-answer routine I learned to follow. On the way to the village square to buy milk or to perform some errand, I would often greet people whom I had not met before—old women hanging laundry in their gardens, or people passing me on the road. I assumed this was respectful behavior in a village and that people would consider me rude if I did not greet them, although I later learned that this was not necessarily true. Invariably after my greeting, the person would peer at me curiously and ask, "Whose are you? (*Pianou eisai;*), to which the proper reply was "the daughter-in-law of Grigoris Yorgakis" (*Tou Grigori Yorgaki i nifi*). An answer that included my name would have been irrelevant, for the question did not ask "Who are you?" Rather, it specifically sought a way to fit the new face into the existing kinship structure of the village. Similarly, when I would be introduced at a social function to a relative of the family, the introduction would consist of a long string of kinship terms (e.g., This is the brother-in-law of the man who baptised Eleni—you remember Eleni? the sister of your mother-in-law's godson?) and no name for the person. These connections seemed complicated to me, yet I came to understand that for the villagers, such introductions were an important way of making sense, a kind of sense in which kinship is the fundamental unit of meaning, and the name of the individual is secondary.

The role of *nifi* had important implications for the research. As a family member, I was able to gain in-depth knowledge of family life that would not have been available to me had I been only a researcher. Roles and responsiblities were assigned to me that fit me into existing family structures, enabling me to see family dynamics from an insider's perspective. By helping daily with childcare, meal preparation, and farm labor and by participating in social and religious events as a nifi, I gained access to most of the family and community contexts in which informal education took place.

There were, however, limits to my participation, some based on my gender and others on my identity as a highly educated outsider. Implicit boundaries on the roles and types of activity expected of me became more overt when I "breached" these expectations by taking on inappropriate roles.[2] For example, my working in the fields evoked protests on the order of "You'll get your hands dirty" (*Tha lerothoun ta heria sou*), "The sun will burn you" (*Tha se kaei o ilios*) , and "You'll get tired" (*Tha kourasteis*).

---

[2]The term *breaching* is taken from the sociologist Garfinkel (1967), who believed that by violating expected patterns of behavior one can discover more explicitly the rules of that behavior. This became one of the tenets of the school of sociology known as *ethnomethodology*.

Figure 8. Katerina and some neighborhood children pose for a photograph with the author.

Telling people that I enjoy working outdoors and don't mind getting dirty and hot did nothing to calm them. Explaining that participation in this work would help my research, as I would learn what is that farmers here have to know, softened the protests somewhat, for example, "Well, if it's for your work . . . " (*An einai yia tin dhouleia sou* . . .) . Complaining that I was being treated as a stranger or guest (*kseni*) rather than as a member of the family produced great embarassment, for I was challenging their sense of honor (*filotimo*). [3] Usually this complaint ended with their accepting my participation at least for the moment. In these situations, informants were reacting to what for them was a basic incongruity: One does not get a higher education and then proceed to work in the fields, even occasionally. In fact, for many Greeks of peasant background, the purpose of getting an education is precisely to leave farm labor behind forever.

Although I insisted on the farm labor issue, I accepted implicit designations of spaces that were off limits because of my gender. The two village coffeehouses (*cafeneia*), for example, were male domains. Although I had to enter one of them frequently because the post arrived there, it was clear from the stares and whispers of customers that I was extremely conspicuous. I would leave as quickly as possible, lingering only if a family member (always male) were there. In Trikala as well, the *cafeneia* were places for men only. If I were shopping in town with my nieces and we needed to stop for something to drink or eat, we would never enter these establishments. Instead we would go to a *cafeteria*, a relatively new social space in Greek towns and cities that attempts to create a European atmosphere. Girls and women are, in theory at least, supposed to feel comfortable entering the *cafeteria* to drink coffee either alone or, more typically, in groups. In practice, however, these spaces too carry overtones of gender roles that Greek girls and women (and by extension, foreign ethnographers) cannot afford to ignore. Although we used the *cafeteria* as stopping off points for refreshments during the day, to spend more time there or to go at night usually meant one was trying to be seen by young men and was interested in developing a sexual relationship.[4]

There were also times, most often when I went running in a small park near the village or walking by myself on the dirt roads that bordered the fields, when I did not fit any prescribed role by village standards. These were the times when I was most saliently a foreigner (*kseni*) who did odd things that a woman from the village would not do. When I asked my family what people would think or say about my running or walking alone,

---

[3]The Greek concept of *filotimo* (honor) has been the subject of much research (e.g., Campbell, 1964; Gilmore, 1987; Herzfeld, 1980; Peristiany, 1966).

[4]Cowan (1990) elaborated more on the differences between the *cafeneion* and the *cafeteria,* with in-depth discussion of the gender issues inherent in the use of these spaces.

their responses indicated that although these activities were not normal for a local woman, the fact that I was from outside made them acceptable. The running was frequent enough that people grew accustomed to it, but the walking always drew curiosity and comments from those outside the immediate family. It was not the walking as much as the fact that I enjoyed doing it alone that perplexed people. They wondered if I wasn't afraid, asked if I wouldn't be lonely, and sometimes interpreted my behavior as a sign of depression.

The issue of reciprocity is a common concern among people who do extended anthropological fieldwork. Although in some cases one can negotiate an agreement to pay the informants a regular sum, this was not acceptable in my situation; my informants would have been extremely offended had I even offered. However, I continually looked for a solution that would preserve their sense of honor (*filotimo*) and my sense of fairness. Finally toward the end of summer, as the weather began to turn cold and Katerina griped about the inconvenience of the old wood stove that would have to be brought in, I knew what I could do: have a heating system installed in the house. This contribution was acceptable to the family where cash was not. We called in a plumber, and within a month the system was finished and for the first time, the whole house (as opposed to just one room with woodstove) could be kept warm in winter.

ISSUES OF METHOD

Throughout fieldwork, I collected several distinct types of record. These included fieldnotes, audio and video recordings, classroom observations,[5] and structured and unstructured interviews.[6] The audio and video recordings form the core of the data. They also typically raise questions about obtrusiveness and prediction that I address here.

Some believe that bringing any form of modern technology into a traditional community is wrong. Reasons for this stance usually point to the disruption of a traditional way of life, a particular group's beliefs about the power of an image to capture a soul, and/or the inevitable self-consciousness that people feel when they are first aware of being recorded.

---

[5] I observed and audiotaped five sessions of the village kindergarten between September and December 1986. In the class were several of the neighborhood children I had been following since April. Most importantly, I was there on the first day of class, which for many children was the first school experience of their lives. Even though schooling was not the focus of this study, I wanted to familiarize myself with the contexts of both informal and formal learning situations.

[6] Twenty-seven individuals were interviewed during the last 2 months of fieldwork. The structured interview appears in Appendix D.

This latter reason is a form of the "observer's paradox," which presents ethnographers with the dilemma of wanting to gather naturalistic data while knowing that the mere presence of an observer (particularly with tape recorder or video) changes the situation and thus the informants' behavior from what it would be without an observer.

Although there may be communities into which it is unwise to bring recording machinery, situations should be evaluated individually. One must consider the nature of the community and also the purpose of the study. First of all, how traditional is traditional? Kiriakitsa is hardly the same as an Indian village in the Amazon jungle. It is close to an urban center, almost every household has a television, most have telephones, and some people own cars. Tape recorders and video cameras evoke curiosity but do not lie outside the realm of the known world.

That they are obtrusive is undeniable. However, the level of obtrusiveness changes as people grow accustomed to them. At first my recordings were full of comments about the machinery and performances and displays for the unknown Americans who would, participants assumed, see and hear them. These comments and performances tapered off however, particularly among the informants I saw daily. I made a point of carrying the tape recorder with me whenever possible even if I was not recording, and the video camera too, although to a lesser extent because of its bulk. In some cases I encouraged informants to handle and operate the machines themselves. The audio recorder was small enough to be carried most places. The video recorder, a Sony 8mm camcorder, was considerably larger, heavier, and more fragile. It also required good lighting and enough distance between camera and subject so that the lens framed the subject (the typical rooms in older village houses were too small). These limitations made the videocamera less flexible than the audio recorder, but it was nonetheless an invaluable research tool.

The focus of the study virtually required machine recordings because informal teaching and learning is a communication process involving at times both verbal and nonverbal language. Demonstration, observation, and imitation may play as important a role as verbal communication (recall the doorbell scene in chapter 1) or may even occur without verbal communication, thus the importance of video recording. Audio recording was sufficient in situations constituted by verbal activity, as for example when a child's pronunciation was corrected. In both audio and video recordings, the second-by-second details of interaction that the analyst can revisit repeatedly make possible the fine-grained analysis that can help us understand how people teach and learn informally. Without these technologies, the study would not have been possible.

Because I was mainly interested in recording activities that involved instruction, I had to develop ways of predicting when these activities were likely to take place. This proved to be difficult, for the predictions were at best probabilistic and intuitive. Often I would realize that somebody was teaching something, but by the time I either turned the machine on or brought it to the scene, the episode would be over. In many cases I missed the beginning and recorded only the body of an episode. These recordings were still useful provided I could remember and write down how the episode had started (i.e., who had initiated and how). The real challenge was finding a way to make recording less chancy. Here careful observation and review of fieldnotes helped because I was able to find certain patterns. I found that teaching and learning were likely to occur when two or more people were engaged in play or in a mutual task, and close enough physically so that they could communicate easily (i.e., not at opposite ends of a watermelon field). Between any two people there is bound to be some asymmetry; if not due to age, gender, educational background, or some other social difference, each person at least has different areas of expertise. Very often in play or at work on a task, what begins as a mutual agreement to play or to work together will shift temporarily to a teaching and learning situation because some difference in expertise has been revealed, and this difference is in turn problematic; that is, the play or work cannot proceed until the more expert person has shared his or her knowledge with the novice.

Thus, I sought out situations in which people were playing or working together in close quarters and tried to have the recording equipment ready or even operating throughout in the hope that some teaching and learning would occur. As predicted, it often did. This covered most of the situations in which some form of physical or physical/verbal activity was being taught. As for the teaching and learning of nonphysical things (e.g., how to be polite, how the kinship system works), I simply had to be present and ready to record in hundreds of conversations — at mealtimes, during visits to and from neighbors and relatives, during car trips, and anytime people were talking. As a result of this constant search for useful material, I recorded far more hours of interaction than I could use. I expressed my frustration over this often enough that Katerina eventually developed a routine that began whenever she saw me leave the house with tape recorder or videocamera in hand:

K. Are you going fishing again? (*Pas yia psarema pali?*)
R. Yes (*Nai*)
K. Good luck! (*Kali epitihia!*)

Figure 9 illustrates the ways I approached the object of study, informal teaching and learning. The first category consists of direct observation of teaching and learning occurring spontaneously among informants. These data form the heart of the study and are the most valid source of

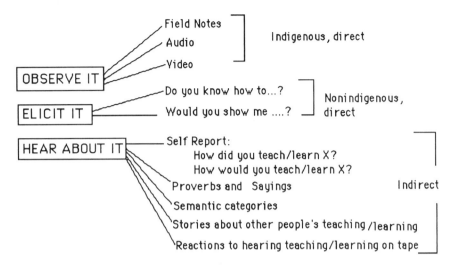

Figure 9. Ways of approaching informal teaching and learning.

information about the ways people in this community teach and learn. In the second category are various kinds of elicitation. Sometimes when I thought things were going badly I would try to elicit informal teaching and learning in which either I would play the role of learner, or I would encourage others to take on the roles of learner and teacher. One afternoon, for example, when Katerina was rolling fillo dough and her 14-year-old granddaughter Kalliope was watching I asked Kalliope, "Do you know how to do that?" This resulted in the granddaughter being given a brief lesson by Katerina (see Figure 10). The episode was clearly not indigenous; had I not elicited it, it probably would not have occurred. Katerina was a master fillo roller, but I never saw her spontaneously teach this skill to anyone else. Several nonindigenous episodes like this are on audio or videotape, and although they do not constitute valid data about informal teaching and learning as it occurs naturally in the community, they do reveal important differences between indigenous and nonindigenous episodes.

In the third category are a number of indirect sources of information about teaching and learning. Sometimes I would ask informants to reflect on how they had learned a particular skill (e.g., "How did you learn to be an apple farmer?"). Almost invariably the answer was "I would watch/see" (*Evlepa*). As is the case in most self-reports, particularly when the processes one is reporting are largely unconscious, the report is not necessarily an accurate reflection of what actually happened. Although observation often plays a key role in the process, other teaching and learning strategies often accompany observation even though the informant may not remember them. Nonetheless, such reports do provide valuable information about

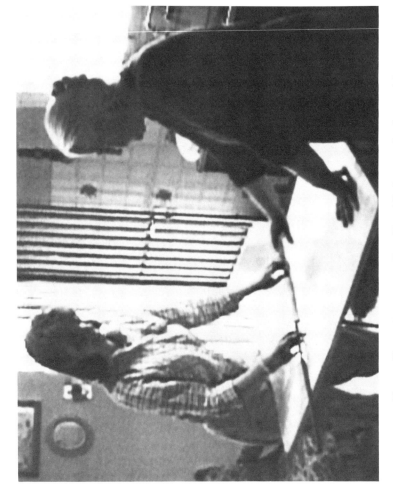

Figure 10. Kalliope tries rolling *fillo* while her grandmother assists.

52

perceptions of and attitudes toward informal teaching and learning. Other indirect sources of information are proverbs and sayings that in some way reflect on informal teaching and learning, or education more generally. One example is the saying, "With whichever teacher you sit, such are the letters you will learn" (*Me opoion dhaskalo tha katseis, tetoia grammata tha matheis*).

Semantic categories are another indirect source, allowing the researcher to learn how the informants classify various aspects of knowledge and education.

> The analysis of a culture's terminological systems will not, of course, exhaustively reveal the cognitive world of its members, but it will certainly tap a central portion of it. Culturally significant cognitive features must be communicable between persons in one of the standard symbolic systems of the culture. A major share of these features will undoubtedly be codable in a society's most flexible and productive communication device, its language. (Frake, 1962, p. 30)

In Greek the words "teach," "learn," "lesson," and "student," for example, all derive from the same root, *math-*. "*S'ematha na odhigeis*" means "I taught you to drive." "*Ematha horo*" means "I learned how to dance." "*Piga sto mathima*" means "I went to the lesson/class," and "*Eimai mathitria*" means "I am a female student in elementary or high school."[7] The fact that the Greek language uses one root to express these four educational concepts, where English uses four different roots, may indicate that for them these meanings are, in word as well as thought, one whole.

Anecdotes and comments about other people's teaching and learning also provided attitudinal information. In one family, for example, the children had not begun talking as early as the children in another family. Another family attributed this late onset of talking to the ignorance of the parents and grandparents and the perception that "They don't talk to the children."[8] From this we learn that villagers perceive children's abilities as not entirely innate, and that talking to children is considered by some an important part of language socialization. In this case, the parents and grandparents were blamed for unwittingly delaying the development of the children.

I gathered one more type of indirect information about informal teaching and learning through one of the questions in the structured interview. In this question, I played for the interviewees a brief teaching and learning

---

[7]A different word, *fititis/fititria,* is used to refer to students in post secondary education.

[8]In fact they *did* talk to the children, so the perception is not entirely accurate. The difference may lie more in the ways they talked to the children. I noticed that in this family, children were not often treated as equal conversational partners. Most of the talk to children consisted of directives and scoldings.

episode in which a grandmother corrects her grandchild's pronunciation. I then asked the interviewees to tell me what happened as though I had not been there or heard the tape. The responses are revealing in several ways. The verbs and verb phrases used to express the action of the grandmother show varying ways of conceptualizing the teaching act, from a discrete speech act such as, "She tells him to say it right" (*Tou leei na to pi kala*) to a more global concept such as "She shows him the correct road." (*Tou dheihnei to kalo dhromo*) . In some cases the respondents also commented evaluatively on the way the grandmother had handled the situation. Some applauded her action—"That's how it should be done" (*Etsi prepei*)— whereas others criticized her for a variety of reasons, for example, "She corrected one mistake, but then she said another mistake," (*Dhiorthose to ena lathos, alla istera tou eipe k'allo lathos*).[9] By eliciting responses to a particular teaching and learning episode, I was able to validate that informants did indeed view this as a form of instruction and to document some of their very different ways of describing that instruction.

The integrated use of these approaches to informal teaching and learning insured that a system of checks and balances operated in my interpretive process. Consistent and intensive field observation enabled me to judge the typicality or atypicality of particular events recorded on tape. Thus, for example the fillo rolling episode was determined to be atypical, as well as nonindigenous. On the other hand, reviewing audio or videotapes often forced me to correct field observations of the same events. From some of the elicited episodes in which I was the learner, I experienced what it might feel like to be a learner in this community and could then measure my experience against the experience of a learner in an indigenous episode. Proverbs and sayings, which tend to reflect only the most stereotypical attitudes, were sometimes borne out by actual practice, sometimes not. These varied sources of information allowed me to triangulate the findings and strengthen the validity of my interpretations.

---

[9]This referred to the fact that she had used a dialect form in a subsequent utterance and thus was inconsistent in her modeling.

4 *Alitheia* and *Psemata* (Truth and Lies)

> *Psemata, psemata,*
> *ftaio ego pou s'ematha*
> *na perpatas stis yeitonyes*
> *na les pos s'agapo . . .*
>
> Lies, lies
> it's my fault that I taught you
> to walk in the neighborhoods
> and say that I love you . . .
> —From a folk song

THE STRUGGLE (*O AGHONAS*)

One way to characterize differences between one cultural group and another is to examine the relative salience of certain themes — themes common to the human condition but nonetheless receiving greater emphasis in a particular society.[1]

In Greece the theme of struggle pervades many everyday conversations. In formulaic greetings, the standard "How are you/What are you doing?" (*Ti kanete;*) is often met with a shrug of the shoulders and "Eh — what to do — I struggle" (*Eh — ti na kano — aghonizomai*) or the more cryptic, "Struggle, struggle" (*Aghona, aghona*). These answers, although they refer primarily to an ongoing situation in the individual's life, are also rooted in

---

[1]Such themes have also been referred to as *configurations* (Benedict, 1934).

55

the past. When questioned about the assumption that life is a struggle, Greeks often begin citing their recent political history—400 years of Turkish domination, World War I, the Balkan Wars, World War II, the Greek Civil War, the British and King Constantine, the Junta, and finally since 1974, something approaching democracy. The implication is that with such a history of domination by foreign powers, one cannot help but see life as a struggle. In the words of Melina Mercouri (1988), Minister of Culture, "We were born in this magnificent country which is to be magnificently cursed. To be Greek is to have this curse" (p. 22). One learns to suspect the motives of others because history has shown that even close relatives may turn against one, as was particularly the case in the Greek Civil War. The political and personal worlds are closely intertwined in Greek life.

A political consciousness emerges early in Greek children, surrounded as they are by the political debates of their parents and other family members. At 4, Alexis already knew the names of the candidates in both local and national elections, and could engage in an early form of political debate in which he said of the candidates, "He made a mess of it for us" (*Mas ta'kane mouskema*) or "He says it well" (*Ta leei oraia*). He was encouraged in this kind of dialogue by adults, who questioned his opinions regularly.

In her ethnography of Vasilika, a village in Boetia, Friedl (1962) noted the same pervasive theme of struggle: "From their earliest days, the upbringing of children plunges them into the role of agonist, and skills for functioning in this fashion are acquired in all stages of a child's development"(p. 76). One way in which these skills are acquired, Friedl said, is through teasing; children at the suckling stage may be offered the mother's breast and then pushed away several times before they are finally allowed to nurse. According to Friedl, this is only the beginning of a long series of similar teasing incidents in early childhood that lead to a recognition that other people's actions and words should not be taken at face value. They "may learn to love and respect their elders, but it is not required that they trust them completely" (p. 80). The desired result of this attitude is that the child becomes guileful or cunning (*ponyiros*), a trait that is considered necessary to a degree among Greek adults in that it equips one to carry out the struggle.

The theme of struggle, although common throughout Greece, has differing regional interpretations. In Thessaly, an individual copes not only with the struggle inherent in being Greek, but also with the onus of being from Thessaly, which has the reputation among Greeks of being a backwater inhabited by uneducated and ignorant people. These attitudes, although no longer well founded, did at one time have an historical basis. Thessaly remained under Turkish control until 1881, 60 years longer than the more southern parts of Greece. During the Turkish occupation, a feudal system operated in Thessaly, with large pieces of land called *tsiflikia* belonging to the Turkish military. The Thessalians became the serfs in this system, and in the words of one author, "The lack of education had sunk the Greek people into a profound darkness of ignorance" (*I ellipsi paidheias eihe vithisi ton Elliniko lao s'ena vathi skotadi amatheias*) (Papadimou, 1980, p. 32). Even when, toward the end of the Turkish occupation, there began to be a spiritual reawakening in Greece, "The plains areas, for the most part, continued to live under conditions of lack of education and ignorance. Few schools functioned, and those that did had teachers with very elementary grammatical knowledge" (*I pedines periohes, sto megalitero pososto, exakolothousan na zoun kato apo sinthikes apaidhefsias kai amatheias. Skoleia litourgousan elahista kai me daskalous me poli stiheiodeis gramatikes gnoseis*) (p. 33).

As recently as 1961,[2] Sivignon wrote of the "backwardness" of Western Thessaly, having conducted a study using demographic indicators including literacy rates, fertility rates, standard of living, number of physicans and hospital beds, and acceptance of innovation. Sivignon said part of the explanation for the "backwardness" may be ethnographic:

> The most backward part of Western Thessaly, a plain between Karditsa and Trikala, is inhabited by Karagounis. . . . They wear a folk costume that can be seen nowadays in the markets of Trikala and Karditsa. . . . The area where the Karagounis wear this folk costume corresponds to the area that is lagging behind with a higher fertility rate, greater number of illiterate people, and so on. (Sivignon, 1976, p. 57)

Although much has changed since 1961, attitudes linger on. Even today, Greeks from other regions consider Thessalians uneducated and ignorant. In 1986, the year this study was conducted, the rate of illiteracy for Greece was reported to be 24.2%.[3] In an informal survey among seven neighborhood households (23 adults) in the community I studied, 26% of the adults were illiterate.[4] Thessalians say they face discrimination when they seek jobs outside the region. The regional dialect, as well as certain nonverbal behaviors, mark Thessalians for quick identification among Greeks from other areas. In fact, the origin of the term *Karagounis* is popularly explained in relation to nonverbal behavior. As one informant explained, when Alexander the Great first came into Thessaly looking for soldiers, he asked the men, "Will you come with me?" In response he received only head movements — head moving up for "No" and head moving sideways (some-

---

[2]The study was conducted in 1961, but the article I quote from was published in 1976.
[3]Greek National Television (ERT 2), September 8, 1986.
[4]I defined *illiteracy* as not being able to write more than one's name, nor read a newspaper.

Figure 11. An elderly widow sits outside her home while her laundry dries (photo by Panos Panagos, 1991).

58

times rocking back and forth) for "Yes." From then on he called these people the Karagounides—*kara* meaning "head" in ancient Greek, and *kounao* meaning "to move."[5]

Greeks sometimes explain this behavior by saying the Karagounides are "lazy from the great heat" (*tembellides ap'tin poli zesti*). More likely, nonverbal signs for yes and no were used to facilitate communication across large distances, for it is easier to see a gesture than to hear a voice. When the distance between two people is too great for a head nod to be visible, community members often amplify the gesture by using the arm; thus "no" becomes a full upward swing of one arm in addition to the upward head movement.

Despite the so-called "backwardness" of Thessaly, the Karagounides have always been able to feed themselves and maintain a viable agriculture, even during times of war. This was a major accomplishment considering the fate of many other regions of Greece. In the more mountainous regions, where the soil is rocky and difficult to cultivate, people lived a more nomadic lifestyle, not subjugated to the Turks to the extent that the Karagounides were, but also far less stable. Not surprisingly, most of the later emigrations of Greeks (to Australia, the United States, Germany, and Sweden) consisted of people from regions other than Thessaly.

Drawing together these various strands of information, a picture emerges of the Karagounides as a farming people who have been dominated by foreign powers for centuries, more so than many other Greeks. Their subjugation has excluded them, until recent years, from the process of formal education they so highly value. They have as a result been labeled *ignorant* by fellow Greeks, and the labels remain even though the initial reason for the label is gone. Regional dialect and characteristic gestures continue to mark them. The struggle has a particular local poignancy because they have done well for themselves in many ways. They have passed their agricultural skills on from generation to generation, maintaining a viable lifestyle and stability. They place high value on formal education, seeing it as a way out from the peasant life and an opportunity to better their situation. On the other hand, they are not reflectively aware of the value of their own everyday teaching and learning even though historically their survival depended on this form of knowledge transmission.

---

[5] There is disagreement among Greek scholars about this interpretation of the etymology of *karagounis*. For one thing, the verb *kounao* is Modern Greek, so it seems historically impossible for it to be attached to an ancient Greek noun. Other interpretations include a Turkish–Greek blend, *kara* meaning "black" in Turkish, and *gouna* meaning "fur" in Greek. However, the *Karagounides* are not known for wearing fur. A third interpretation is all Turkish, with the second part roughly corresponding to the word in Turkish for "Greek", so we have "black Greek." However, the *Karagounides* as a group are rather light-skinned (Papadimou, 1980).

The salience of struggle (*aghona*) as a cultural theme made Thessaly a particularly interesting region for research on informal teaching and learning. If we can assume that patterns of face-to-face interaction reflect deeper cultural themes,[6] then it should not surprise us to find that informal teaching and learning in Thessalian family and community contexts reflects the wider theme of struggle. Cultures tend to display some degree of coherence such that themes or patterns emerging at one level "resonate" throughout the system.[7] In the rest of this chapter and those that follow, I examine precisely *how* the theme of struggle is reflected and constructed in everyday learning situations.

In trying to understand how informal teaching and learning is carried out in a small, cohesive community like this one, I was consistently struck by the distinction participants made between *alitheia* and *psemata* (truth and lies, according to the dictionary definitions in Pring, 1982). For the participants, as well as for any observer, it was important to know first of all whether the activity being pursued was "for real" (*alitheia*). When a 14-year-old girl is asked to make Greek coffee for her grandfather, she knows that the activity is for real (i.e., she is expected to produce a drinkable cup of coffee). The teaching that her grandmother provides is structured with this shared assumption in mind. Each step must be done properly, and none can be left out. On the other hand, when a 4-year-old girl and her 7-year-old sister go with their parents to the fields, they are given child-sized tools and rather than working alongside the parents to produce real "work," they are directed to the open space between two fields, where they imitate the parents' activities. In both cases, teaching and learning are involved, but the participants structure the activities very differently because one task is framed as *alitheia* and the second as *psemata*. I wanted to explore how these different sets of expectations structure teaching and learning interactions, for the distinction is meaningful not only at the microlevel in informal teaching and learning, but also at a macrolevel involving the broader cultural system and the theme of *aghona* (struggle) discussed previously.

The *alitheia/psemata* distinction functions as a framing device in informal teaching and learning. Frames are sets of expectations that tell participants or onlookers in an activity how to interpret its meaning (Bateson, 1972; Goffman, 1974). For example, moviegoers usually know not only that the movie is not real life, but also whether it is comedy, drama, adventure, or some other form. These frames structure the way the

---

[6]Heath (1983) and Scollon and Scollon (1981) provided interesting discussions about the relationship between cultural values and patterns of communication.

[7]The notion of resonance across different levels within a culture is taken from Metraux (1953, cited in Leichter, 1979).

audience interprets the movie. Similarly, *alitheia* and *psemata* frame participants' expectations about the way the activity is going to be carried out and the ways in which actions are to be interpreted. They have the effect of channelling learning and teaching in one direction or another. Both directions can further learning, but they do so in very different ways. Chapters 5, 6 and 7 examine how learning is furthered differently in the two frames. First, however, I turn to the local, everyday meanings of *alitheia* and *psemata* in order to establish the context for the upcoming chapters. Specifically, what do these terms mean to children in this community, and in what contexts do they hear and use this distinction?

PSEMATA AND *ALITHEIA* IN EVERYDAY DISCOURSE

In actual usage among villagers and townspeople, *psemata* and *alitheia* take on several shades of meaning that literal translations (i.e., truth and lies) fail to capture. In order to understand the network of meanings surrounding these words, I have examined discourse contexts surrounding everyday uses of one or both words and have attempted to link *psemata* and *alitheia* to related concepts that help us understand their power. As Bakhtin (1981) pointed out, "It is precisely in the process of living interaction with this specific environment that the word may be individualized and given stylistic shape" (p. 276)

The sequences of dialogue that follow illustrate different contexts of the *alitheia/psemata* distinction. A brief discussion of the situated meaning follows.

Example 1

Dina (Household 3), two of her children, and I are sitting in Dina's front yard chatting. Dina's 5-year-old son Yiannis appears from the road with his grandfather. Yiannis runs over to join us, and says that he has had an ice cream.

R. Bravo, how good your grandfather is, eh, that he gives ice cream
(*Bravo, ti kalos einai o pappous eh pou dhinei pagoto.*)

D. Lies, he didn't eat
(*Psemata, dhen efage*)

Y. I ate
(*Efaga*)

D. He didn't eat
(*Dhen efage*)

Y. Look I ate it   since I ate it   I ate
(*Na to efaga   afou tofaga   efaga*)

The word *psemata* is used here to mean lie or falsehood, in keeping with the usual literal translation. This illustrates that the Greek word does map over the English concept of lie or falsehood. The difference is that the Greek word also has a range of other meanings not entailed by the English word.[8]

Example 2

Thomas and Alexis (father and 4-year-old son) are sitting close together on a couch in their home. Thomas is playing a guitar and intermittently singing; Alexis is holding a child-sized guitar and listening to his father sing. Thomas begins a popular song, changing the name at the beginning from "*Maro Maro*" to "*Tzano Tzano*," which is one of Alexis' nicknames.

T. Tzano Tzano, youth comes once. . . .
(*Tzano Tzano, mia fora ta neata . . .*)

A. The standard one
(*To alithino*)

T. . . . don't send me away now that I found you
(*. . . m i me dhiohneis tora pou se vrika*)

A. The standard one
(*To alithino*)

T. So, shall I sing it now in standard form? Without *Tzano*?
(*Lipon, na to po tora stin alitheia; horiz Tzano;*)

A. Yeeees
(*Neeee*)

T. *Maro Maro* youth comes once (Alexis bounces with rhythm)
(*Maro Maro mia fora ta neata*)
That's how the standard one goes. It's *Maro Maro* . . .
(*Etsi leyetai to alithino. Einai Maro Maro . . . .*)

In this example, the context suggests that the meaning of the word *alithino* encompasses the real thing as opposed to a fake, the original as opposed to a later version, and the accepted standard as opposed to a personalized version.

---

[8]Whether or not Yiannis did or did not actually eat an ice cream is not known.

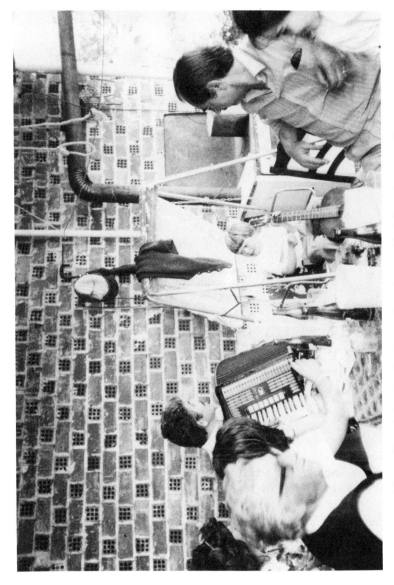

Figure 12. Alexis "plays" guitar and watches as his father plays accordion.

Example 3

Alexis is playing with his grandfather Grigoris on the grandparents' bed. It is evening and Alexis is going to sleep at the grandparents' house. His grandmother, Katerina, has been trying to get him to the bath but he has been more interested in playing with his grandfather. He tests his grandma's tolerance a few times, calling her a *fourada* (mare) and other derogatory names.

K. Let me get a nettle, to get a nettle now, you'll see
   (*Yia na paro mia tsouhnida na paro mia tsouhnida tora tha eideis*)

G. Ah you *tsoglanara* (pet name of Alexis)
   (*Ah vre tsoglanara*)

A. you give —
   (*mou din —*)

G. We'll put it on the penis here   bring the scissors
   (*Na t'vazoume sti marika edo   fer'to psalidi*)

K. Outside I'll get a nettle and tsak tsak
   (*Exo tha paro mia tsouhnida kai tsak tsak*)

G. Rosy, bring the scissors over here, here bring the scissors here, the scissors
   (*Rosy, fer'to psalid edoyia ap'edo fer'to psalid ido to psalid*)

K. No!
   (*Ohi*)

A. Eh No!
   (*Eh ohi*)

G. Quick, quick
   (*Grigora, grigora*)

K. No!
   (*Ohi*)

A. Grandmaaa (A. is ready to cry)
   (*Yiayiaaaa*)

K. No no   I won't allow   Rosy   no no no the scissors
   (*Ohi ohi dhen afino ego Rosy mi mi mi to psalid'*)
   Let's go so I can wash you
   (*Pame na se plino ego*)

G. Ah you silly one I'm kidding you and you're afraid
   (*Ah re boubouna se kano psemata go kai si fovasai*)

K. Ha ha ha he's looking at Rosy to see will she bring them or not
   (*Ha ha ha kitaei kai ti Rosy na di tha to fer' then tha to fer'*)

G. What little lips are those you have, man (to Alexis)
   (*Ti hilakia ein'afta pou eh's re*)

K. Rosy won't give them to him, silly one, he's kidding
   (*Dhen to dinei i Rosy vre hazeh psemata leei*)
G. What little lips are those you have, what are those my pasha
   (*Ti hilakia ein'afta pou eh's, t'ein afta pasia'm*)

Here the word *psemata* refers to what in English we would call kidding or teasing. The grandparents have both made mock threats to Alexis, and he has been taken to the edge of real fear. They do not want him to go over this edge, however, and so the words *se kano psemata* (I'm kidding/teasing you) are used to reframe what has gone on up to this point. Alexis can thus back away from the possible interpetation that this is *alitheia* and forego (albeit gradually) his fearfulness.[9]

Example 4

Alexis himself uses the word *psema* in similar fashion when I reprimand him one afternoon for frightening a hen in a neighbor's yard by chasing it and waving a stick at it. "To kano *psema*," he replies. Literally, this means "I make it lies" but again the meaning is more accurately translated as "I'm just teasing/kidding it."

Example 5

In a scene that is microanalyzed in chapter 6, Alexis watches and partici-pates while family members perform several rounds of "cupping," a healing procedure common in Mediterranean countries. The procedure is somewhat frightening in that it requires a flaming torch. Alexis' father, Thomas, having finished cupping Alexis' mother, threatens to do Alexis next. The child is scared and cries beside his mother until his father leaves the room. A few minutes later, Alexis calms down and his father returns, this time to coach Alexis in cupping his mother. However, mother, father, and child all agree first that this will be *psemata*:

T. Like that, play/fake, eh?
   (*Etsi psemata, eh;*)

---

[9]This interaction will for some readers bring up questions about the grandparents' wisdom or lack thereof in teasing a 4-year-old boy about doing damage to his genitals. As an ethnographer, it is not my position to make value judgments about cultural practices, although admittedly I was surprised when I first noticed behavior like this in Greece. To my informants, however, such behavior is a form of harmless play. I believe that the informants' meaning system must guide any outsider's interpretation, and so, unless the informants themselves have conflicting notions of what this means, we have no choice but to accept their interpretation as the "true" one for them.

A. Ah, yes
   (*Ah, nai*)
T. OK
   (*Endaxi*)

Here *psemata* is used to mean "play," and in this case specifically play that omits aspects of the real cupping process (i.e., the flame and accessories) that would be dangerous for a 4-year-old to handle.

Example 6

One afternoon Alexis is playing outside with a 7-year-old girl named Maria. Maria picks up a hose with sprinkler attached and starts to sprinkle water over Alexis' tricycle. Katerina, Alexis' grandmother, says to Maria, "*Ela Maria. Leme na kanoume kanena psema, alla ohi hazomares teties*" (Come now, Maria. We say to make a few lies/to play some tricks, but not such nonsense). Here Katerina calls attention to the fact that *psemata* (in the sense of teasing, tricks) are expected and even encouraged, but that there is a line beyond which these tricks become "nonsense." She does not articulate what the line is, for it is more a function of situation that of any overriding principle. The message is that one has to be sensitive to the situation to gauge the appropriateness of a particular trick.

These examples show that the meanings of *alitheia* and *psemata* cover a range, from the literal (and probably still the core) interpretation as truth/falsehood, to the more situated interpretations as real/fake or play, original/later version, standard/personal version, and trickery or teasing/straightforward.

CONCEPTS RELATED TO *PSEMATA* AND *ALITHEIA*

Friedl (1962), whose ethnography of a Greek village was mentioned earlier, pointed to a relationship between the teasing behavior she described and the general theme she saw as pervasive in the Greek culture — that of the *aghona* or struggle. Life is seen as a struggle in which one must try to overcome the forces that militate against happiness and success. Through childrearing practices that involve teasing, adults implicitly teach their children to cope with the struggle to come. Children learn not to trust outward signs too easily and to be prepared for rebuffs and disappointments.

The limitations of my own fieldwork do not allow me to posit a direct causal relationship between practices of childrearing, which I observed directly, and general cultural themes, which I can only infer. Certainly the *aghona* theme is real, and childrearing practices such as the one Friedl described exist, but it is not possible in ethnographic work to show direct causation. However, certain interactional patterns I observed among children and between children and adults do seem to support the resonanace of the theme of struggle at different levels.

At the local and family level where I worked most intensively, *the alitheia/psemata* distinction is part of a cluster of related concepts, mastery of which is considered an important step toward adulthood. This cluster forms part of what individuals need to know in order to behave as functioning members of their society (Goodenough, 1957, p. 167). Among other things, individuals need to learn how not to accept surface appearances, how to doubt, how to be skeptical of others; they need to be skilled at teasing and yet not allow others to tease *them* too much; they need to gain expertise in taking advantage of social situations for the benefit of themselves or their families but not allow others to take advantage of *them*; and finally, they need to know that outside of the inner circle (which usually means the nuclear family) nobody is to be trusted, for "everyone has his or her own interests at heart" (*Oloi kittan ta simferonta tous*).

Such caveats may seem universal to many of us; after all, don't we all need to know these things? What is there about this social knowledge that is particular to the context of this study?

One answer lies in responses to an interview question in which informants were asked, "How do you know if a child (before school age) is very smart?" Although most referred generally to the "way of speaking," two informants elaborated a bit more:

Interviewer: How do you know if a child (who hasn't gone to school yet) is very smart, or a "match" as they say?
(*Pos xerete an ena paidhi (prin akoma paei skoleio) einai panexipnos, i "spirto" pou lene?*)
Respondent 1 (elderly man): He contradicts/goes against
(*Paei anapodho*)
Respondent 2 (woman in her 40s): You go to tease/trick the child, and he or she says "no".
(*Esi pas na to xeyelaseis to paidhi kai sou leei "ohi".*)

In both of these responses (given during separate interviews), it is the skeptical child who is considered smart, the child who does not immediately accept what adults say. Among some groups, such behavior might be labeled *disrespectful*, but in Kiriakitsa and Trikala, it is labeled *smart*. The second respondent alludes to the notion that it is acceptable practice for adults to use tricks (*psemata*) to lure a child into demonstrating his or her cleverness.

The function of *psemata is* further revealed in a dialogue between Alexis and his grandmother concerning my presence in the house. I had gone running early in the morning, and when I returned, Alexis was on the porch with Katerina. Alexis, with a gleam in his eyes, said to his grandmother, "She wasn't sleeping" (*Dhen kimotan*). She replied "I didn't know" (*Dhen ixera*).

Before I had left for my run, I had told Katerina where I was going. Apparently she had then told Alexis that I was still sleeping. Alexis was proud that he had caught his grandmother lying to him. Katerina did not appear embarassed or apologetic at all. In fact the lie continued in Katerina's feigning of ignorance. It didn't matter to either of them that the lie was caught, for it was used to *facilitate the moment* (i.e., to prevent Alexis from going in my room, keep him quiet, or prevent him from running out to look for me). Now that the moment was over, the lie was no longer important as an evasion, only as a game of cleverness. In this interaction, both the liar and the discoverer of the lie had a chance to shine. The liar could outwit the other temporarily, and then the discoverer could use his wits to show up the liar. Both individuals won.

In another interaction during a family lunch, Katerina actually instructed Alexis to be aware of being teased by his father, Thomas, and to respond in kind:

> T. Do you hear you'll sleep outside tonight, there; don't be afraid
> (*Akous tha pas exo tora apopse ekei mi fovase*)
> A. Why—? (Alexis' mother laughs)
> (*Yiati—;*)
> G. Kid who runs into things (colloquial expresssion)
> (*Traka*)
> K. Alexi, your Dad is laughing at you/taking you in
> (*Alexi, se yelaei o babas*)
> N. (unintelligible)
> K. Dad is taking you in, silly; why should I go outside, say
> (*Se yelaei o babas haze yiati na pao exo pes*)
> A. Ah man leave us alone/give us a break over there
> (*Ah mare parata mas ap'ekei*)
> K. Hah!

Community members are ambivalent about this kind of cleverness (*ponyirada*). On the one hand, they see the need for it in order to get along in Greek society, but on the other hand, they claim it is not right. As one informant stated, "Children learn first the clever/cunning way, and later the right way" (*Ta paidheia mathainoun prota to ponyiro, kai meta to sosto*).

All of the qualities and abilities mentioned so far—cleverness, cunning, the ability to tease and take advantage as well as to catch the teasing of others, the ability to know the *psemata/alitheia* distinction and to use it to one's advantage — overlap a concept that is central to the *Trikalinoi* (Trikala residents') experience. This is the concept of *mangya,* which figures prominently in a folksong about Trikala. A term that does not have an exact translation in English, *mangya* has been alternately described as cleverness, cunning, or street smarts, yet it is more than the sum of these parts. Rena, an 18-year-old girl, one day pointed out to me that she had rolled her socks down "so that my legs will look longer" (*yia na fainounte pio megala ta podia mou*). When I laughed, she added, "That's what it means to be a Greek, smart, a mangas!"(*Afto tha pi Ellinas, exipnos, mangas!*).

The concept of *mangya* is controversial. Twenty-eight respondents to an interview question were divided as to whether it was a positive or negative quality.[10] To some it is an insult to be called *mangas,* whereas to others it is a compliment. In order to be a *mangas,* one must among other things acquire an ability to (a) display oneself as X when one is really Y, and (b) perceive other people's displays and not be duped. Whether or not one considers *mangya* a positive quality, one still has to be clever enough to protect oneself along the lines of (b). This passive and often unacknowledged form of *mangya,* as well as the more active form, are both contingent on mastery of the *psemata/alitheia* distinction and the meaning system that surrounds it. A child who grows up in this community, then, acquires the *psemata/alitheia* distinction as a piece of a complex whole.

SIGNALS OF *PSEMATA* AND *ALITHEIA*

Both *psemata* and *alitheia* framing occur in procedural, declarative, and discrete-point modes of instruction. Although the *alitheia* frame is, in Goffman's terminology, a primary frame and therefore does not need to be signaled in any special way, the *psemata* frame is a transformation and must be signalled. Goffman (1974) called this signaling process *keying.*

Community members signaled the *psemata* frame in a variety of different ways, from very explicit cues to far more subtle ones. Sometimes several cues would appear in clusters, and other times only one would occur. Following is a list of the cues I found:

---

[10]Ten said it was positive, 9 said it was negative, and 9 said "both" or "it depends." When asked on what it depended, some said it was only acceptable among intimates; others said it was unacceptable for educated people; others said it was only acceptable toward children; and others distinguished between "real" *mangya* and *psefto* (pseudo) *mangya,* the former being positive, the latter negative.

1. The most explicit is *naming the frame*. Thomas does this in the cupping episode when he says, *"Psemata,* eh?" Any grammatical form of the roots *psema* and *alitheia* can be used to explicitly name the frame. There are also other words and phrases that can can be used instead, such as *paizo* (I'm playing), *kano plaka* (I'm making fun), *mangepses* (you have become a *mangas*), and *se yelaei* (he or she is tricking you). The frame can be named before it begins or in retrospect.

2. *Role play* (participants taking on roles of others outside of the interaction) and *role switching* (participants trading roles with each other) can also signal the transition from *psemata* to *alitheia* or vice-versa. When an individual pretends to be someone else and marks the transition for others, it is like saying "This is play" (Bateson, 1972). Role switching can be accomplished through an overt statement, such as "I play the teacher, you play the student," or less overtly through future and conditional verb forms. For example, when Alexis wants his grandmother to pretend she is in another village (because in his game of "busdriver" he has let her off in the village Megalohori and she has not yet returned), he says to her, "You wouldn't talk" [because you are pretending to be in Megalohori] (*Esi dhen tha milouses*). Role play and role shift can also be signaled through a change in social or regional dialect, such as when an Athenian mimics a village dialect or the reverse. Finally, role play and role switch can be cued through voice changes, including changes of intonation, pitch, speed of speech, rhythm, and volume.

3. The *psemata* frame can be signaled by the use of certain *objects* as well as by the language and behavior of the participants. Toys in general have this function (i.e., a person who is using a toy is usually playing), but in Greece I also noted a special class of toys that I call "baby tools." Children often played with objects that bore certain family resemblances to the tools or instruments their elders were using, but that were smaller or somehow less functional than the grown-up versions. Examples include a child-sized hoe, which children used when they went to the fields with their elders, a small washboard, a piece of wood in the shape of a guitar, a toy guitar, and others.

4. *Laughter* can be another signal of *psemata* frame, although not all laughter necessarily functions this way. When participants are teasing one another, however, laughter often accompanies the propositional content of the teasing.

5. Finally, certain questions that I call *"teasing questions"* can signal the *psemata* frame. In these questions, the speaker knows the answer or at least has an opinion; the speaker also knows that the listener lacks information to answer the question fully yet will try anyway. Rather than seeking information, the questioner attempts to reveal the learner's state of knowledge.

In keying a strip of activity as *psemata,* a "systematic transformation" must occur (Goffman, 1974, p. 45), and we should be able to find evidence of this transformation in the interaction itself. There should be indications not only at the boundaries (or *rim* to use Goffman's term) of the *psemata* frame, but also internally. In the analysis that follows in the next three chapters, I compare strips of interaction within episodes framed as *alitheia* and *psemata.* Chapter 5 examines two strips of procedural teaching, dancing (*alitheia*) and cupping (*psemata*) and briefly describes other episodes of these types. Chapters 6 and 7 follow the same format: Chapter 6 compares two strips of declarative teaching, babyclothes (*alitheia*) and kinship (*psemata*), and chapter 7 compares two strips of discrete-point teaching dealing with language use—em ti (*alitheia*) and trapezi (*psemata*) (see Table 2).

These episodes were chosen on the basis of several criteria. One was to limit the range of participants as much as possible. For this reason, all but one episode, babyclothes, involve the same learner, Alexis. Another criterion was the type of record. I preferred to use videotaped episodes if available; if not, audiotape was acceptable. Other criteria were quality of recording, and the prototypicality of the teaching/learning episode, based on the features of prototypicality outlined earlier.

Because so many of these microanalyzed episodes involve Alexis, it is appropriate here to comment on the typicality of these episodes and on the uniqueness of this child. Alexis was a "commuter" in that he lived both with his parents and sisters in Trikala and with his grandparents in the village. His time was divided approximately equally between the two settings. His grandmother also frequently took care of him in Trikala during the morning hours when his mother was busy in the beauty shop. Thus, Alexis had characteristics of both village and town children. His language resembled that of the village children, but his expectations about the availability of toys resembled those of an urban child more closely. When the village children played in the road or in the yards, Alexis often joined them. At times he was somewhat of an outsider in the other children's games, but it was hard to tell if this was due to his younger age or his semi-urban life. Another child of the same age, Vangelis, often seemed equally at sea in the older children's games.

TABLE 2
Framework for Microanalysis of Episodes

	Alitheia	Psemata
Procedural	Dancing	Cupping
Declarative	Babyclothes	Kinship
Discrete Point	Em ti	Trapezi

Because the focus of the microanalysis is teaching and learning situations, it is useful to study one learner in order to better understand the range of instructional situations an individual encounters. In the following episodes, a number of different teachers have an influence on Alexis, including grandparents, parents, sisters, an older cousin, and some plumbers who are working on the house.

5 Teaching and Learning to Do

In this chapter, I examine two episodes of procedural teaching and learning. The first, dancing, is framed as *alitheia,* and the second, cupping, is framed as *psemata.* The discussion of each episode includes foreshadowing commentary, vignette, and interpretive commentary. This is followed by a comparison of the two episodes, briefer descriptions of other procedural episodes, and a summary. Those readers who would like to go directly to the data will find transcripts of these episodes in Appendix E.

DANCING

Dancing is a key activity in many Greek religious events, as well as in traditional celebrations and more modern outings to *tavernas*[1] on weekends and evenings. Weddings and baptisms are usually followed by large celebrations that include food, wine, and dancing. The Easter celebration usually includes dancing as well. Participants in dancing may include all generations, from old people to very young children. To be considered a good dancer, one must be able not only to follow the steps in circle dances such as the *kalamatiano, sirto,* and *tsamiko,* but also to lead a circle (which requires considerably more skill, self-confidence, and a certain air of *savoir faire*) and to perform a solo dance called the *zembekiko.*

---

[1] *Tavernas* are establishments that serve food, wine, and beer and also provide music (either live or recorded) for dancing on weekends and special occasions. In Thessaly, they tend to be located slightly outside of the major towns.

Traditionally the *zembekiko* was a man's dance, but now women occasionally perform it too. In the *zembekiko,* the dancer innovates within a range of movement genres whose basic form is circular; the dancer moves his feet from side to side, keeping his arms outstretched and moving rhythmically, sometimes snapping his fingers. Occasionally the dancer dips down to touch the floor or his feet with one hand, or innovates special hand and arm movements. Unlike other Greek dances, the *zembekiko* does not have a prescribed sequence of steps, hence its value as a measure of individual skill and creative expression. Throughout the individual *zembekiko* performance, close family members and friends squat in a circle around the dancer, clapping and cheering the dancer on with *opa's,*[2] whistles, and other expressions of high spirits (*kefi*) and appreciation.

Children are included in dance events starting at a very early age. One of the first dances a child might witness is the one occurring at her own baptism celebration where, although generally too young to participate,[3] the child is nonetheless one of the centers of attention. She witnesses her father, mother, and other adults who serve as role models dancing and receiving praise for their skill. Thus, from the start, children see dancing as a way of not only building family and community solidarity through the cooperative circle dances, but also demonstrating individual ability and increasing one's status within the group by leading circle dances or performing a *zembekiko.*

Alexis is no exception; his mother, father, sisters, and grandfather are all recognized as good dancers, so it is reasonable to infer that he is highly motivated to become a good dancer himself. In the vignette that follows, Alexis' grandfather instructs him in some elaborations of the *zembekiko.*

Alexis' *Zembekiko*

It is the evening of December 4, 1986, in the kitchen/bedroom of Alexis' grandparents' home in the village. Alexis is going to spend the night, which he does several times a week. He and his grandfather are dressed for bed in pajamas, and Alexis' fold-out bed (an armchair in the daytime) is prepared. I have just put a new cassette of Greek music on my tape player for Grigoris to listen to, and Alexis begins dancing on the bed almost as soon as he hears the music. Grigoris, sitting at the kitchen table, begins to engage with his

---

[2]*Opa* is a term of encouragement, somewhat similar to *olé* in Spanish.

[3]Children are sometimes baptized as late as 3 or 4 years old, in which case participation in the dancing becomes a possibility.

grandson's dancing, and I run for the videocamera (as usual, slightly after the beginning of the event).

The event includes three songs. Throughout these songs, Grigoris sits at the kitchen table, facing Alexis, who dances on the fold-out bed. Grigoris claps his hands in time to the music, showing enthusiasm and encouraging Alexis. He soon addresses Alexis, saying, "Bebi,[4] do like this too," (*Bebi, kane k'etsi*) and clapping under his own knee at the same time.

Alexis is more concerned at first with where the music is coming from, as he cannot see the cassette player. He asks several times, "Rosy, what's making the music?" *(Rosy, ti kanei ti mousiki;)* and eventually I respond by gesturing toward the cassette player.

Meanwhile, Grigoris continues to clap his hands, trying to attract Alexis' attention. After a few moments, Alexis does turn and face his grandfather and again Grigoris shows him the under-the-knee clap, saying, "Hey, do like this" (*Yia kane etsi*) . Alexis watches this time, but still does not try to imitate. Grigoris then claps his hands normally and says, "Hey, do the handclapping too" (*Yia kane kai ta palamakia*) . This Alexis imitates several times, and when Grigoris again shows him the under-the-knee clap, he imitates that as well. In fact, he claps under his knee three times, looking very pleased with himself, and laughs, "Ha, the big leg!" (*Ha, tin podhara!*).

Grigoris then introduces another move, circling the hands, saying "Do like this too" (*kane k'etsi*) as he demonstrates. Alexis picks this up almost immediately and adds his own innovation, circling the thumbs only, which Grigoris then imitates.

Grigoris and Alexis continue in this way through a series of elaborations on the *zembekiko,* including moving the hands in and out, moving one hand like a wave, moving both hands like a wave, falling down and getting up, and using the worry beads. Some of these variations are introduced by Grigoris and some by Alexis. Now and then Grigoris breaks into singing along with the music.

The first time Alexis falls is probably accidental, for one of the legs on the fold-out bed has just collapsed, creating a sloping "dance floor." When he falls, he does not get up immediately; instead, he lies flat on his back and makes a siren noise, to which Grigoris responds by bringing a cup of water from the table and sprinkling Alexis' head with a few drops. Alexis gets up,

---

[4]It should be noted here that "Bebi" is Alexis' pre-baptismal name. All Greek babies are called Bebi/Beba until they are baptized, which can be as late as 3–4 years (Alexis was baptized at the age of 3). Grigoris still sometimes uses this earlier name for his grandson, as well as a variety of other names and nicknames. It may be significant that in this instance he chooses a "babyish" name.

wipes the water from his face, and says, "Thank you, Grandpa, you're good" (*Efharisto Papouli, eisai oraios*). Grigoris replies, "You're good, you're good" (*Eisai kalos, eisai kalos*). Apparently the "cure" for the "accident" worked wonders.

Alexis then falls twice more. But these second and third falls appear to be on purpose, and possibly imitative of the near falling motion used by some expert *zembekiko* dancers.

The last variation, the use of the worry beads, is introduced by Grigoris, who hands the beads over to Alexis, saying, "Now play the worry beads" (*Yia paixe kai to beghleri*). Grigoris encourages him with a rhythmic chant, intoning, "dang dang diggy diggy dang dang dank," and accompanying Alexis is a series of *'opa's* which mark his enthusiasm.

At the end of the third song, Grigoris, who has been growing less active, turns to me and says, "Turn it (the music) off now, it's enough" (*Kleis'tin tora, ftanei*).

Interpretation

In the interpretation that follows I investigate four questions. These same questions also guide the interpretations for the other five episodes.

1. How is initiation accomplished, and by whom? (i.e., initiation of teaching/learning and, in *psemata* cases, initiation of *psemata* frame)
2. How is the task or knowledge system structured, and if the episode is framed as *psemata,* how is the task or knowledge system transformed?
3. What is the nature of the instructional interaction?
4. What is the relation between the learner's zone of proximal development and the teaching?

Initiation.   Alexis initiates the dancing, which is clear enough evidence of his interest. The first overt initiation of teaching and learning, however, does not occur until Grigoris claps under his own knee and says to his grandson, "Bebi, do like this too." It takes several attempts before Grigoris actually succeeds in getting the child's attention, so initiation can be said to occupy several turns. Initiation is not successful until Alexis turns and faces his grandfather and begins responding to the directives. By the time Grigoris says "do, do" (*kane, kane*),the initiation is complete and the teacher and learner can be said to have established a shared focus, which is a prerequisite for teaching and learning to begin.

Between the beginning and completion of initiation, Grigoris tries several

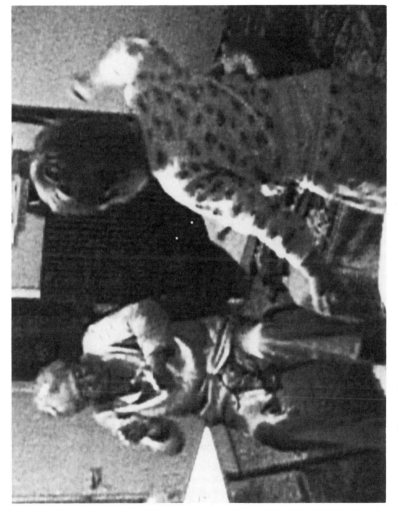

Figure 13. Alexis does the *zembekiko* with instruction from his grandfather.

strategies to get the child's attention. His first utterance, "Bebi, do like this too," includes a vocative attention getter (Bebi), a directive (do), a deictic expression (like this) which refers to Grigoris' simultaneous model, and a coherence marker (too) which indicates that clapping the hands under the knee is part of a larger behavioral pattern, not just an isolated action. Grigoris' next utterance, "Listen, come here," while it includes two directives, is oriented more toward getting the child's attention than toward teaching him. His third utterance, "(*Yia*) do like this," includes a directive (do) and a deictic expression (like this), but no longer any vocative or direct address. He does however include the discourse marker *yia*, which often precedes directives in Greek. His fourth utterance, "Do, do" is only a directive.

What we see in Grigoris' speech, then, is a gradual progression in which functional elements of communication are added or dropped in accordance with the child's listening and performing behavior. When the first utterance fails to get the child's attention, Grigoris drops the teaching directive and uses an attention getting device only. As the child turns and faces his grandfather, the attention getter becomes unnecessary, so in the next utterance Grigoris drops this element and reintroduces the teaching directive and deictic expression. In the final initiating utterance, Grigoris reduces the verbal communication to directives only.

Grigoris also attempts to get the child's attention through nonverbal communication. He claps under his knees three times before he succeeds. Unlike the verbal component of initiation, the nonverbal component is relatively stable across attempts; Grigoris does not, during this initiating section of the interaction, reduce or change the nonverbal model in accordance with Alexis' listening and performing behavior.

Although this initiation takes only 17 seconds, it is an intricate process involving the interplay of several verbal attempts of varying complexity coupled with nonverbal modeling on the part of the teacher, and verbal and nonverbal responses on the part of the learner.

Task structure.   The dance consists essentially of two kinds of movement: (a) a basic, continuous, circular movement in which the body remains upright and the weight is shifted from one foot to the other in rhythm to the music; and (b) elaborations on this basic movement, occurring at irregular intervals (but still of course in rhythm with the music). These two kinds of movement can be likened to a basic drum beat, continuous throughout a piece of music, and melodic variations introduced at irregular intervals.

In the video recording of the scene, the following variations appeared:

1. clap hands under knee	(G introduces, A imitates)
2. circle hands	(" " " ")
3. circle thumbs only	(A introduces, G imitates)

4. move hands out one at a time   (G introduces, A imitates)
5. move one hand like a wave   (A introduces)
6. move both hands like a wave   (A introduces)
7. fall down/get up   (A introduces)
8. use worry beads   (G introduces, A imitates)

Although these actions are linked through chronological order in real time, they are also linked through a different kind of order. The task itself (dancing the *zembekiko*) is hierarchical, with some elements of the task subordinate to others. A cognitive model based on the theory of activity would involve various embeddings, as illustrated in Figure 14.

According to the model of activity current in the work of Soviet psychologists such as P. I. Zinchenko (1979), aspects of a task that are singled out of the overall task and overtly taught (as is under-the-knee clapping) are at the level of action. When subtasks are no longer overtly attended to, they drop down to the automatic level and are called *operations*. Once we have learned something, in other words, it becomes automatic in the sense that we no longer need to pay specific attention to it unless a problem arises. A model such as this is useful in portraying what, at a given instance, is being overtly taught. At a later point in Alexis' development of dance, the components that were actions in this scene would probably have dropped to the level of automatic operations.

Instructional Interaction.   Grigoris plays the role of teacher and monitor of Alexis' dancing. In several instances, he expands the child's repertoire of

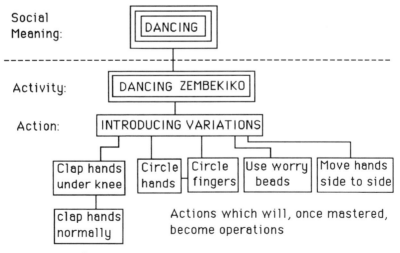

Figure 14.   Levels of activity in the *zembekiko*.

variations or elaborates on how to perform a variation, such as the clapping under the knee routine. Alexis plays the role of learner, as well as that of an already competent dancer who nonetheless recognizes that he can learn more.

Grigoris teaches Alexis through both verbal and nonverbal channels, telling his grandson what to do and showing him as well. The verbal and nonverbal channels occur simultaneously, and both perform important instructional functions. Without the nonverbal modeling, the verbal directives would have little meaning since they are attached to deictic expressions such as "like this" which require referents that the listener can perceive. "This" refers to the nonverbal modeling taking place at that moment.

It is interesting to note, however, that Grigoris never models with his whole body, only with his upper body. Thus, the modeling that he does is only partially iconic with the desired behavior. This partial iconicity does not seem to pose any problems of interpretation, however, for the elaborations he is teaching are mainly functions of the upper body anyway.

As we saw in the discussion of the initiation, Alexis does not immediately become engaged in the teaching/learning process. Grigoris' initial attempts to engage him are met with questions directed to another focus, the source of the music. Once Alexis does become engaged, however, he begins to imitate his grandfather's actions quite closely. These imitations can be viewed as proximal indicators of learning. Clapping under the knee is a particularly good example, since in the beginning Alexis is not able to do this, but after the grandfather has "scaffolded" the activity by getting Alexis to clap normally, the child succeeds in clapping under the knee. Figure 15 enables one to see more graphically how the verbal and nonverbal behaviors of both participants are related in real time. Of particular interest is that *opa* serves not only as a marker of enthusiasm but also as a marker of the transition from one type of movement to the next.

I noted earlier that Grigoris' verbal behavior changes continually in the initial phase, whereas his nonverbal behavior (the periodic motion of clapping) remains relatively constant. Most of his adjustments to the learner are made verbally. This suggests a functional relationship between the two channels, such that the verbal channel is used to carry out scaffolding, whereas the nonverbal channel is used to provide the model of expected behavior. When the task is easier than clapping under the knee (such as moving the hands in and out), Grigoris does not provide any verbalization, relying on modeling alone to teach Alexis. Thus, when skills are easy or have already been practiced, nonverbal communication may assume the full teaching function, whereas more difficult skills or new skills may require a functional separation of teaching into verbal scaffolding and nonverbal modeling.

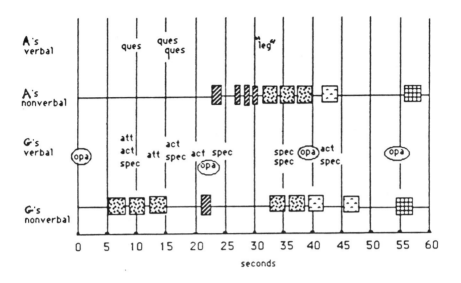

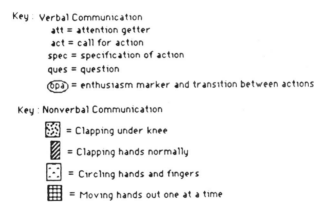

Figure 15.   Relationship of verbal and nonverbal activity.

Relationship between Learner's Zone of Proximal Development and Teaching.   Although Alexis performs some of the dance elaborations with ease, and even initiates some himself, he has trouble with the first one, clapping under the knee. Grigoris recognizes this and adjusts his teaching accordingly. Rather than insist on clapping under the knee, he breaks the task down into the simpler component, clapping the hands normally. Once Alexis has picked this up, the grandfather reintroduces under-the-knee clapping successfully.

This interaction combines elements of both scaffolding and shaping.

Grigoris has held the ultimate task constant, but has simplified it at a certain point by reducing the degrees of freedom with which Alexis has to cope at any one moment. However, he does not allow Alexis to remain on the simplified level; once the child is comfortable with handclapping, Grigoris re-introduces the under-the-knee clap. In other words, Grigoris uses shaping very sparingly; the rest of the time his modeling and verbal directives provide, without simplification, the help that enables Alexis to complete the task. It is this type of instruction (both the scaffolding and shaping) that is referred to in the literature on everyday cognition as "proleptic" or within the zone of proximal development. In this view, what the child can do *with* help is the real indicator of his or her development.

CUPPING

Cupping (*vendouzes*) is a healing practice common in the Mediterranean (in French *ventouses* and in Italian *ventosas*), whereby a healer "draws the cold out" (*Vgazei to krio*) . The person who has a cold, flu, or cough lies on his or her belly with the skin of the back exposed. The healer works with four to six thick-rimmed glasses,[5] rubbing alcohol (or strong ethyl alcohol), matches, and a fork whose tines are wrapped in cotton. The cotton is dipped in alcohol and lit so that the fork becomes a small torch. Holding this in one hand, the healer takes a glass with the other hand, inverts it briefly over the flame, then quickly attaches the rim of the glass to the sick person's back. Because the flame inside the glass has created a vacuum, a suction seal is formed and the skin rises in a dome under the glass. The procedure is repeated until all the glasses are attached to the back. Then the healer begins rotating the glasses, setting up a rhythmic pattern punctuated by the sound of the suction seal being broken. Sometimes a dark circle appears temporarily on the person's back where a glass had been. Cupping continues for anywhere from 5 to 15 minutes, after which the patient is briefly covered with a wool blanket. The next and last step is a rubdown (*entrivi*) with alcohol, lasting only a minute or so. Then the healer covers the patient again with the blanket and the process is complete.

In the vignette that follows, the focus is on Alexis' experiences as a learner, and particularly on what he experiences as the action moves from Part 2 to Part 3, for it is here that a major shift in framing occurs — the shift from "the real thing" (*alitheia*) to "play" (*psemata*).

---

[5]Special glasses made for this purpose can be bought. From the base they flare out into a bulb shape, then close in about one third from the top, and flare out again in the upper third.

Alexis as Healer

The cupping event that I observed and participated in took place on November 26, 1986, toward the end of my fieldwork, in the Sakkas family home in Trikala. Participants were Nina, her husband Thomas, and their children Kalliope (14), Alexis (4), and myself. There were four major shifts in participation structure, and the roles that each of us played are shown in Table 3.

Cupping is a frequent practice in the Sakkas household, so Alexis is no stranger to the rather dramatic sights and sounds it entails. During Part 1, he is highly excited and eager to observe closely. He makes a number of comments about people's roles, for familiar people are behaving differently from what he has come to expect. In the following sequence, Alexis addresses me, telling me about his mother's role:

A: ". . . as if she were the man — like — like she has you as her wife and she takes vendouzes" (. . . *san na itane andras — san — san na s'ehei yineka kai sou pernei vendouzes*).

N: "Do you know why he says that, Rosy? Because Thomas cups me, you see. He thinks that only the man cups the woman" (*ksereis yiati to leei, Rosy; yiati o Thomas mou pernei vendouzes, vlepeis. No-meizei oti mono o andras kanei vendouzes sti yineka*).

He also notes the role reversal of Kalliope and me, in that up until this time he has only seen me operating the videocamera. If Kalliope has taken on my role, then I must be in Kalliope's role, as he points out when he says, "They don't call her Rosy, they call her Kalliope" (*Dhen tin lene Rosy, tin lene Kalliope*).

He is also especially aware of and fascinated by the fire, saying at one point to his mother, "Mama, don't burn me. If you burn me, you won't

TABLE 3
Major Shifts in Participation Structure

Part 1	Part 2	Part 3	Part 4
Nina cups RH; Alexis watches; Kalliope works video; Thomas in other room.	Thomas cups Nina; Kalliope lights matches; Alexis tries to light matches; RH operates video.	Alexis cups Nina; Thomas coaches Alexis; RH operates video; Kalliope in other room.	Nina cups Alexis; RH operates video; Thomas & Kalliope in other room.

have a little boy" (*Mama, mi me kapseis. A'ma me kapseis, dhen tha eh's paidhaki*).

In Part 2, Alexis becomes more interested in participating, so he chooses to bring his father the matches as needed, for the "torch" goes out from time to time and has to be relit. However, Kalliope is faster and more expert with the matches than Alexis. He is left standing several times with arm outstretched and unlit match in hand, offering a match to his father, who takes one from Kalliope each time instead. The tension builds with each offer[6] in the following progression:

1. A. "Here Babouli (affectionate form of 'Daddy'), here you are." (*Edho Babouli, na to*)
2. A. "I have it." (*T'oho eyo*)
   T. "Never mind, you can do it later." (*Dhen birazei, tha to kaneis argotera*)
3. A. "Are you (pl) going to blow me up (exasperate me) now?" (*Tha me skaste tora;*)
4. A. "What are you, man?" (*Ti'se si, re?*)
5. A. "I'm mad." (*Eho nevra*)

At this point Thomas, who by now is finishing the rubdown, gestures with his hand toward Alexis' face — a threatening gesture. Alexis returns the gesture to his father.

In the transition from Part 2 to Part 3, Thomas comes around to where Alexis is standing, picks up the child and places him face down on the bed beside his mother. Alexis, believing he is about to be cupped as well, screams in terror. Thomas goes out to the living room and sits down to smoke a cigarette, while Nina comforts Alexis on the bed for a minute. Alexis then goes out to the living room and comes back a few moments later with his father. Nina, who is still lying on the bed, says to Thomas, "Leave him be, Thomas, to play a little" (*As tone Thoma, na paiksei ligo*).

Thomas then helps Alexis climb onto his mother's back to straddle her, and says to his son, "play, eh?" (*psemata, eh;*). Alexis then begins to play at cupping his mother, using one glass (as opposed to the six that Nina and her husband used) and the fork but no flame, while Thomas stands beside him and coaches. After a few minutes, Thomas leaves the room, and Alexis continues to "cup" his mother; he also engages in a dialogue with me about bringing matches:

---

[6]There are many offers because by now they are using *cipporo* instead of rubbing alcohol, having run out of the latter. *Cipporo,* the locally made drink distilled from grape must, is not as strong as rubbing alcohol; thus the flame goes out more frequently.

A. (pointing to bookshelf) "There, there, there are the matches, the real ones." (*Ekei, ekei, ekei ein'ta spirta, t'alithina.*)

R. "I have here." (holding out pretend match) (*Eho edho.*)

A. "The real ones." (*T'alithina*)

Alexis shows great delight during the interaction, both while his father is present and after. When he finishes the cupping, he gives his mother a rubdown without alcohol, imitating the movements he had seen his father do, and ends by saying to his mother "You're ready" (*Etimi eisai*).

In the transition from Part 3 to Part 4, Nina cuddles Alexis on her lap and he comments on his role in the previous round:

A. "As if I were the father and I had you as my wife!" (*San na imouna babas kai s'iha yinaika*)

N. "Why, do fathers do that to their wives?" (*Yiati, etsi kanoun oi babades stis yinekes tous;*)

A. "Yes" (*Nai*)

N. "Yes?" (*Nai;*)

A. "Yes, why did you do Rena (A's sister)?" (*Nai, yiati ekanes sti Rena;*)

N. "You're the little boy and you do his Mama." (*Esi eisai to paidhaki kai kaneis ti Mama.*)

A. "As if I were the father." (*San na imouna babas.*)

Alexis then snuggles closer and pretends he is a baby. A few moments later, Nina lowers him onto the bed and very gently raises his shirt. As she places the glasses briefly on his back (without flame or fork), she asks him. "Does it burn, does it burn?" (*Kaei; Kaei;*) and tells him to "Be a little patient" (*Na kaneis ipomoni*). He giggles throughout most of this interaction. She follows with the rubdown; as they end the round, Nina wishes her son "get better soon" (*perastika sou*) and coaches him to say thank you. Then he climbs into her lap again for a few more moments of cuddling.[7]

Interpretation

Initiation. Although Alexis has been an observer of the cupping process in the first two parts (he has watched Nina cupping me and Thomas cupping Nina), overt teaching does not begin until Part 3. Certainly Alexis may have learned a great deal from watching other people cupping and being cupped, but there is no evidence that the model they provided was intended or taken as a teaching model. Even when Nina calls to Alexis several times at the beginning of this segment, there is still no evidence of teaching. It is possible

---

[7]The transcript (Appendix E) shows the segment of cupping in Part 3 from before Thomas enters the room until just after Thomas has left.

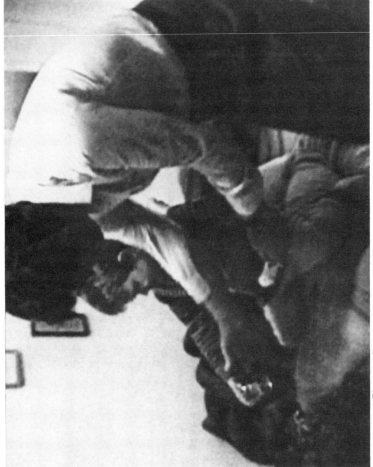

Figure 16. Alexis tries cupping his mother with help from his father.

at this point that Alexis could simply climb onto his mother's back and play at cupping without any instruction from his father.

The first overt indication of an intent to teach occurs when Thomas says to his son "Get up here" (*Aneva edho pano*). This is followed shortly by many more directives, which taken together with Alexis' responses provide evidence of a mutual intent to teach and learn.

The initiation and establishment of the *psemata* frame is a little more complicated. The first overt indication that this will not constitute actual cupping comes when Nina, summoning Alexis, says, "Not fire my child, come" (*Ohi fotia, paidhi mou, ela*). In other words, one of the major components of the cupping process is going to be omitted. Immediately after this, Nina addresses her husband: "Leave him be a little Thomas, to play so I can get up" (*As ton ligo Thoma, na paixei yia na sikotho*). Here the framing is referred to through the verb "to play." Thomas, shortly after entering the room, contributes to the firm establishment of the frame when he says to his son, "Like that/this, play eh?" (*etsi psemata, eh;*).

The deictic expression *etsi* (like that/this) can function both distally and proximally in Greek. It is also used to indicate ease of accomplishment, for example when one asks, "How did you manage to fix the motor?" and the response is *Etsi*. One is given to understand that it was no big deal, or that the respondent doesn't want to provide details. *Etsi* in Thomas' utterance probably links the model (which is now distal) with the upcoming (proximal) attempt, which will be *psemata*.

The rising intonation on "eh" indicates to Alexis that Thomas expects a response, either agreement or disagreement, and Alexis indicates agreement with the *psemata* frame when he says, "Ah yes" (*Ah nai*) . Thomas follows with "OK" (*Endaxi*). The framing has thus been confirmed by all three of the main actors in this episode, and from here the action can proceed within the shared frame.

Because overt teaching begins almost immediately after the *psemata* frame has been confirmed, it is likely that establishing the frame was a pre-condition for teaching. Thomas' "OK" (*endaxi*) functions as a transition, closing the frame-establishing sequence and at the same time opening the teaching, as if he were saying "OK, now that we've got that straight I can start instructing you."

Thomas also closes his part in the *psemata* frame with a gesture as he leaves the room—a sort of scooping gesture with the elbow bent and hand moving from about shoulder height down in an arc towards the center of the chest. The gesture is accompanied by a laugh. Together, gesture and laugh indicate, "This is ridiculous."

Task Structure.   In order to understand how the *psemata* frame changes the task structure of an activity like cupping, we must first imagine what the task looks like in an *alitheia* frame. Figure 17 models the cupping process as it took place in Parts 1 and 2, when it was "for real."

As the figure shows, wrapping cotton around the fork, dipping the fork in alcohol, and lighting the match to the fork are all necessary subtasks to creating a torch. The torch in turn is needed in order to create a vacuum in the glasses. The *psemata* version of the task that Alexis accomplishes, however, does not include all of the subtasks pictured here. The most overt transformations involve equipment, namely the omission of fire (matches) and multiple glasses from the process. These, at least, are the omissions that the participants refer to explicitly. Another type of equipment that is omitted, but not referred to overtly as an omission, is the *cipporo* or alcohol used as fuel for the torch. Clearly, all the participants understand that the dangers of a 4-year-old child playing with a flaming torch preclude its use here. Less clear are the reasons for Thomas' attempt to limit his son's use of the glasses. Perhaps he thought multiple glasses would complicate matters too much. In any case, his objection is overridden by both Alexis' insistence (two directives to "bring another") and Nina's provision of another glass (she has three lying next to her on the bed). Thomas also transforms the activity when he holds onto the fork with Alexis to prevent the cotton from falling off. Alexis strongly resists this limitation on his freedom of movement, saying, "Leave me! Let go! Let go!" (*Ase me! Ase! Ase!*).

Because fire is not used, other aspects of the process are transformed. There is no suction when Alexis places the glasses on his mother's back, and thus no sound of the seal being broken when the glasses are lifted. Without suction to bind them to the skin, the glasses balance precariously on Nina's back and often fall over, in one case all the way to the floor. But more importantly, without suction no healing effect on the patient is expected.

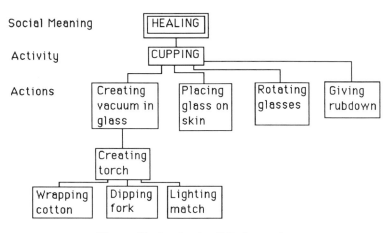

Figure 17. Levels of activity in cupping.

Alexis' process differs from the *alitheia* model in other ways, too, but not as a direct result of the *psemata* frame. He works quite slowly and deliberates a good deal in between moves, also having to replace glasses that have fallen over. Thus, the overall speed and rhythm of the process is different from the *alitheia* version. But these changes could be expected from any novice even if he were older and allowed to use fire.

Finally, we should note the transformations that Alexis makes to compensate for the omission of fire and suction. He refers several times to fire as though it were present. "Eh eh the fire!" (*Eh eh ti fotia!*) is his response to the cotton having fallen off the fork, which, if real fire were involved, would have created a dangerous situation. Alexis also uses sound effects to mimic the sound of the glasses being attached. The imitation is quite different from the real thing, however, sounding more like hissing or burning than suction. When his father leaves the room, Alexis says with dissappointment, "Now—the fire went out." (*Tora ezvise i fotia.*) The word *tora* (now) is spoken slowly, with vowel elongation, heavy stress on the first syllable, and a considerable pause before the next word. These vocal effects in *tora* are used in cases when a speaker wants to indicate not a time but rather a feeling of hopelessness and futility.[8] It is probably no coincidence that Alexis uses this form of *tora* here, for his father, upon leaving the room, has just made the futility gesture. They collaborate in a two-part harmony, Thomas providing the gesture, his son providing the verbalization.

Instructional Interaction.   Each person in this scene has a role to play. Nina's role is to be the "patient" and to provide what is necessary for Alexis to play (i.e., the fork and the extra glass). She also helps establish the limits and rules of the interaction (e.g., that fire should not be used and that pulling down one's mother's pants is unacceptable). Thomas' role is to be the teacher and the monitor of Alexis' process. He also limits, or tries to limit, the extent of Alexis' experience when he tells his son to use only one glass. Alexis occupies the role of central attention and learner. As a learner upon whom certain limits are placed, he tests these limits, and in the case of the glasses, he succeeds somewhat in that he is allowed to play with two glasses rather than one.

In this episode, Thomas teaches mainly through directives that name an action, and Alexis responds for the most part with those actions. In the broadest sense, the teaching is done verbally, while the learning is carried

---

[8]Greeks often cite this use of *tora* when they want to demonstrate how difficult it is for foreigners to learn their language. A favorite anecdote tells of a foreigner at a railway station who asks a Greek whether a particular train has left yet. The Greek, who knows the train left hours ago, replies, *Toooora* and gestures futility or ridiculousness with his arm. The poor tourist, knowing only that *tora* means "now," is none the wiser.

out physically. However, this is only true if we limit our scope of study to this particular strip of interaction. Earlier, we know that Thomas provided a model (however unintentionally) and that Alexis observed closely. Later, we know that Thomas left the room and Alexis continued to participate in cupping, eventually changing roles with his mother so that he became the patient and she became the healer. So Thomas' and Alexis' engagement in the task do not begin and end with this episode. Rather, the episode constitutes the most prototypical part of an extended teaching and learning experience.

Thomas' directives are listed below for easier reference. The verbs are in bold print:

1. *Aneva edo pano* (get up here)
2. *Vale* (put)
3. Ante *vale* (go on, put)
4. *Vale vale* (put, put)
5. *Oraia,* **vale** *alli* (good, put another)
6. *Ela, tin idia tin idia tin idia tin idia, na ti* **valeis** *kai na ti* **vgaleis** *sinehia*
   (Come on, the same the same the same the same, you should put it on and take it off continually)
7. *Ante* **vale** *alli* (go on, put another)
8. *Piase kai to vambaki* (hold on to the cotton too)
9. *Ante* **vouta** *to* (go on, dip/plunge it)
10. *Ah,* **vale** *allo tora, aftin tin alli pou einai edo, aftin* (ah, put another now, this one the other which is here, this one)
11. *Ante* **vale** *pali* (go on, put again)

The verbs are all imperative with the exception of *valeis* (you put) and *vgaleis* (you take off), which are preceded by the infinitive particle *na* and conjugated in second person singular, present tense. This can be roughly translated as "you should + verb."

In addition to his heavy reliance on imperative verbs, and especially the verb *vazo* (put), Thomas also relies on the particle *ante* and on pronoun reference and deictic expressions. *Ante,* which I have translated as "go on," contrasts interestingly with *ela,* translated as "come on." *Ante* is the imperative form of a Classical Greek verb *ago* meaning "to lead." In Modern Greek it is not used in any form other than the imperative. (Sofia Lenetaki, Personal Communication, Feb. 8, 1988.) *Ela* is the imperative form of *erhomai,* meaning "to come," which is still used in all its forms today. Both imperative forms, however, tend to be used as discourse markers more than as true verbs. They precede or follow a call for action in the respondent, and can be used almost interchangeably; where one makes sense, the other makes sense as well. However, there is a subtle difference in terms of perceived politeness, *ante* being perceived as somewhat slangy. *Ante* also tends to place more distance between speaker and hearer, where *ela* tends to emphasize closeness. Not surprisingly, the mother uses *ela* almost exclusively, while Thomas uses *ante*.

Some of Thomas' directives contain nothing but the verb *vale* or *ante* + *vale*. The direct object of *vale* is assumed to be "glass" (in Greek the neuter, *to potiri*) or "glass for cupping" (in Greek the feminine *i vendouza*). Other directives contain direct object pronouns as well, such as "another" "the other" "the same one" and "it," all of which refer to one of the cupping glasses at hand.

Most of Thomas' directives involve "immediately local resources" (Erickson, 1982), making the overall communication quite telegraphic because pronouns and deictic expressions carry a great deal of shared information. There is however some confusion over what *alli* ("another" with feminine ending) refers to. The first time that Thomas uses it, Alexis takes his father's meaning literally as "another cupping glass." Consequently, Alexis responds with the directive, "Bring the other." (Alexis uses the neuter form of "other," which probably means he is referring to the neuter "glass" rather than "cupping glass.") Here Thomas corrects with a string of four "the same's," in feminine form. More confusion over reference occurs when Alexis begins to look for a third glass (he is already using two), and Thomas, who has just told him to "put another now" has to repair by saying "this one the other which is here, this one" and by pointing to the glass already on Nina's back.

In response to Thomas' teaching, Alexis places and replaces the glasses on his mother's back. He has as iconic models the cupping performances done earlier by his mother and father and as a verbal model the directives which his father is giving. He appears to be thinking in between moves, trying to decide what to do next. Often his father's directives provide the stimulus for the next move, though in some cases he also moves independently of the directives.

Because Alexis is concentrating on nonverbal response, he says relatively little during this episode. Several of his utterances, however, provide important information about his learning process:

— Wait so I can get a fork
   (*Stasou na paro ena pirouni*)
— With the fork
   (*Me to piroun'*)
— Bring the other [glass]
   (*Fere t'allo*)
— Eeh eeh the fire, bring another [glass]
   (*Eeh eeh ti fotia, fere k'allo*)

— Leave me, let go, let go
(*Ase me ase ase*)

— Yes yes yes I put it, yes yes
(*Nai nai nai to valo, nai nai*)

These utterances indicate an impatience on his part. He continually wants to do more than his father is directing him to do. He tries to make the *psemata* version as close as possible to the *alitheia* version by including the fork, the multiple glasses, and the fire at least in word if not in deed; he also pushes his father's hand out of the way and asserts that he can manage on his own. He seems to prefer to work independently of his father's overt teaching or even to resent being taught. Teacher and learner do not share the same goals for the activity.

The literature on cultural incongruity, which shows how conflict arises when teachers and learners do not share the same or similar cultural background, implies that cultural congruity should be characterized by an absence of conflict. However, the informal teaching and learning I observed in Greece leads me to a slightly different understanding: Conflict of one sort or another may be present in many kinds of teaching and learning, but conflict over interactional patterns is probably especially characteristic of culturally incongruous encounters. In this community, interactional patterns did not differ enough to interfere with informal teaching and learning. Differences in teachers' and learners' goals, however, did sometimes cause conflict.

Relationship Between Learner's Zone of Proximal Development and Teaching. Although Alexis may not share his father's goals for the activity, he demonstrates a good understanding of the overall task, having observed cupping not only this time but many other times as well. He knows the various components of the process, and can easily identify the missing or omitted ones.

In terms of performance, he is able to manipulate the glasses and use the fork in as real a way as possible, given that fire and suction are not possible. He finds the repeated use of one glass too limiting, and demands two glasses. He also resists his father's physical intervention (holding the fork with him). Later on, he demonstrates rudimentary skill in the rubdown and in the discourse conventions of cupping, saying at the end, "You're ready, my dear mother." In other words, he is able to do everything that his parents, in the *psemata* framework, construe as appropriate, and is anxious to do more. He construes his own potential at a higher level than his father allows for. Thomas provides instruction in timing more than anything else, directing him *when* to place the glasses. With the exception of the timing,

Alexis' activity appears to take place below the zone of proximal development.

In these ways the task is shaped more than scaffolded. The task has been simplified through the *psemata* frame so that it falls well within the abilities of the learner, and the learner can experience success at every point in the process. Although the teacher does provide verbal assistance in the form of directives and at one point, physical assistance (holding the fork), it is not the kind of assistance that enables the learner to complete the real, *alitheia* task.

COMPARISON

The cupping and dancing episodes exhibit a number of similarities. Both involve transmission of skills that are traditional in nature and both carry a good deal of cultural information, the dancing being of course the more public of the two, but also the more strictly Greek of the two. Cupping, although less public, is more widespread across cultural areas, covering most of the Mediterranean. Both episodes involve procedural teaching and learning with certain operations singled out and magnified for the purpose of improving the learner's performance. In both cases, a process is decomposed, indicating the teacher's intention to teach. And finally, both episodes take place within the close, personal world of the family.

The major differences, aside from the tasks themselves, lie in the ways in which the participants structure the tasks. In the dancing episode, when a variation was difficult for the child, the teacher intervened and broke the task down until the child could do it. The teacher's help scaffolded the child's participation in the full (*alitheia*) activity, making it possible for the child to complete the difficult part. In the cupping episode, from the very start, the task was framed as *psemata* and difficult or dangerous parts were explicitly omitted from the activity. The adults consciously shaped the task through *psemata* framing so that the learner could successfully participate in the now-limited version.

OTHER PROCEDURAL EPISODES

Several other procedural episodes deserve special mention here because they illuminate further the range of procedural teaching and learning in the two frames.

Other Dancing

Dancing is taught and learned through several different participation structures. One of these, as we saw in the microanalyzed episode in this chapter, is the one-to-one interaction of adult and child apart from the context of a larger dance event. Another participation structure also involves adult with child, but the interaction takes place within a larger dance event. This was the case in a sequence I videotaped at a baptismal party, where a mother instructed her daughter in a dance called the *tsifteteli* (see Figure 18), which is derived from Turkish belly dancing. Modeling was used to a large degree, this time completely iconically, for the mother was upright and participating fully. Fewer verbal instructions or directives were given because the music was too loud to hear anything but shouting, so most "directives" were delivered nonverbally; for example, the mother would pull the daughter toward her instead of saying "Come here." When the girl appeared shy and reluctant to dance, the mother engaged the help of a playmate of the same age by pulling her into the twosome and indicating with gestures that she wanted the playmate to dance. The playmate complied, briefly, and the daughter danced with her for a few moments.

Children can also learn to dance by participating directly in the adult circle during a dance event. This occurred every time I observed a dance event — marriages, baptisms, and other celebrations. Children from the age of 4 up would hold the hand of the mother, father, or other caretaker and dance within the adult circle (see Figure 19). No particular attempt was made to instruct them in the steps; they were expected to follow as well as they could by watching others and moving with the rhythm. Older children (from about 10 up) are sometimes placed in the lead position, where they show their prowess by doing special and difficult elaborations of the basic dance steps.

Twice I observed a fourth way of learning to dance in which children of varying ages would form their own separate circle during a dance event (see Figure 20). The older ones, being more expert, would provide a model for the younger ones in much the same way as the adults did, but again no explicit teaching took place. Sometimes, in fact, the youngest children were literally dragged along in the circle, unable to cope with any kind of steps at all yet still "dancing" by virtue of the implicit assent to participate that comes when one joins hands in the circle.

In all its forms, dancing seems to be taught in the *alitheia* frame. The task is not simplified or made less than real. When adults model, they model the *alitheia* form, and children and other novices (myself included) are expected to do the best they can. Even without an audience and a surrounding dance event, as the microanalyzed episode indicates, Alexis was expected to dance for real.

The multiple participation structures through which one can learn to dance point to the vitality of this traditional practice. Other traditional skills may slowly die out and be replaced by more modern customs, but

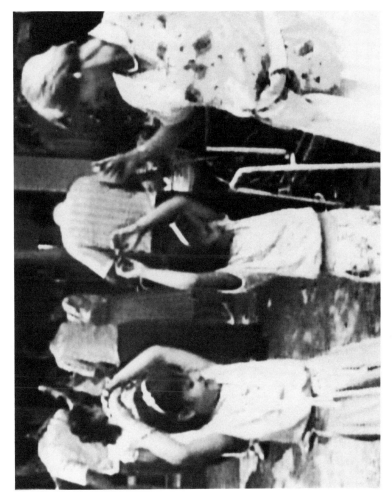

Figure 18. Two girls dance the *Tsiftetell* with encouragement from a mother.

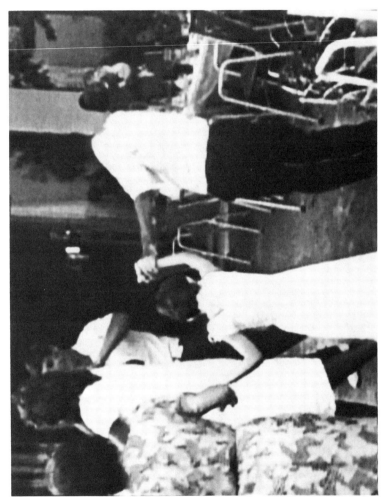

Figure 19. Children often dance in adult circle.

Figure 20. Children sometimes form their own separate dance circle.

Greek dancing is not one of them. Rock and roll, disco, and new wave music are popular among the young people, but rather than threatening the traditional dance forms, they appear to co-exist peacefully with them. Young people learn both, not one or the other. The fact that traditional dancing can be learned in a variety of ways makes it flexible and easily available, thus making its perpetuation more likely than a skill whose transmission is more rigidly controlled.

Making Coffee

In the coffee-drinking habits of modern-day Greeks, there are some interesting parallels to the situation described for dance forms. Two kinds of hot coffee are available almost everywhere in Greece — traditional Greek (originally Turkish) coffee made in a *briki* (a small, narrow-necked pot made of copper, steel, or aluminum) and served in espresso-sized cups with saucers, and *Nes* or instant Nescafe served in a larger, rounded cup such as one sees in the United States. In the *cafeneia,* only Greek coffee is available, but in the more European style *cafeteria* customers can order either kind. In either case, customers must specify with their orders how sweet they want their coffee, for the sugar is added before the coffee is heated; *pikro* (bitter) means one teaspoon; *metrio* (medium) means two; and *gliko* (sweet) means three. To order coffee without sugar is more complicated because the terminological system does not provide easily for that option.

A teaching and learning episode in which 14-year-old Kalliope made Greek coffee at her grandparents' house demonstrates the continuity of this practice in the new generation. Kalliope, who had been told by her grandfather that she was to make the afternoon coffee, was already well versed in making coffee at her own parents' home, so the instruction in this episode focused on measurement (correct proportions of water, coffee, and sugar for four people) and location of the ingredients and vessels. The grandfather dealt mainly with the teaching of measurement, whereas the grandmother helped Kalliope locate the right equipment. The task was not simplified in any way, and in fact both grandparents insisted on accurate and expert performance of this *alitheia* task. They scaffolded Kalliope's role by providing guidance as needed; only at one point, when the coffee and sugar were measured into the water, did the grandmother actually take over the task from Kalliope. Once this was done, however, she returned the task to Kalliope to finish. At the end, as Kalliope began to pour coffee from the *briki* into the four cups, she was reprimanded by her grandfather for not distributing the *korfi* (foam) equally among the four cups. Managing the *korfi* (also called *kaimaki*) is a crucial aspect of expert performance. In fact, the grandparents considered this aspect of the performance so important that they related it to Kalliope's future aspiration to be a flight attendant, asking her, "How can you expect to become a flight attendant if you don't know how to make coffee?" When I pointed out that Nescafe rather than Greek coffee is generally served on airplanes, Kalliope's grandmother replied firmly, "It doesn't matter. That too has to be served" (*Dhen birazei. Servirete k'afto*).

Rolling Fillo

The coffee-making and dancing contrast with this next episode in terms of continuity as well as framing. *Fillo* (the thin sheets of pastry used in baklava and other Greek dishes) is still rolled out at home by many older Greek women, including Kalliope's grandmother. This is a time-consuming process requiring considerable manual dexterity. Shortly before the coffee-making episode, as Katerina was rolling out fillo and Kalliope was sitting nearby, I asked Kalliope, "Do you know how to do that?" This nonindigenous initiation resulted in Kalliope getting up to try rolling *fillo* under Katerina's guidance. However, Katerina overtly framed the attempt as *psemata,* twice in the beginning and once at the end, as follows:

— **Fake,** just so, now I'll give you the roller, you turn from that side
(*Pseftika, etsi, tora tha sou dhoso ego to plasti, yirizeis ap'aftin*)
— Good one, do it there, just **fake,** with the stick . . .
(*Kale na kaneis aftou yia pseftika etsi esi me to xilo . . .*)
— You don't know, go on, do it **fake** now and leave it, don't wreck it . . .
(*Dhen xereis, ante etsi kan'to pseftika tora kai as'to, mi halas . . .*)

In this episode, the *psemata* frame was used for yet another function — marking an activity that is not going to be necessary for the learner to learn. The practice of rolling one's own *fillo* is dying out in the youngest generation of Greek women. It has already disappeared among some of the middle generation, for example Kalliope's mother. When I asked Kalliope if her mother buys *fillo* ready-made from the store, she replied, "No — since Grandma makes it" (*Bah — afou i yiayia to ftianei*). The implication here was that when Grandma is no longer able to make *fillo,* then the family will resort to buying it in a store. Thus, even though Katerina provided scaffolding for Kalliope within the *fillo* episode, it was clear that the grandmother did not expect her granddaughter to carry on this skill.

Working in the Fields

Families within the neighborhood differed considerably in the expectations they held for their children's futures. This was illustrated by the contrast between the Ntiroyiannis and the E. Karagounis families in the roles assigned to children. The Ntiroyiannis family, which consists of grandparents, parents, and three children, took their children to the fields with them on an almost daily basis. While the parents and grandparents worked, the children played nearby or were given child-sized tools so that they could "work" alongside the adults. These tools were another signal of the *psemata* frame; the children were not expected to perform the real task with these tools, but rather to make motions similar to those of the adults, to participate in a child's version of adult work. Unlike the *psemata* framing in the *fillo* episode described earlier, here the children were expected to eventually learn to farm.

In contrast, the E. Karagounis family, consisting of grandmother, parents, and two children, never took the children to the fields; the grandmother stayed home with the children while the parents worked in the fields. The children's mother, Eleni, was emphatic about not wanting her children to become farmers: "Let them become anything they want, but far from the fields" (*As yinoun oti theloun, alla makria ap'ta horafia*). The Ntiroyiannis family, on the other hand, saw farming as one option for their children; if nothing else worked out, they would have that skill.

Acquiring Literacy Skills

The only family in which I saw school-type literacy skills being practiced intensively with small children was the E. Karagounis family. The mother, Eleni, had a 6-year education and was diligent about practicing the alphabet and numbers with her children, Vasoula (8) and Vangelis (4). On several occasions she also asked me to teach the English alphabet and numbers in English. The teaching was procedural more than declarative or discrete point, in that the children were expected to say the letters (or numbers) in order. Eleni recited under her breath as the children recited out loud, and modeled out loud if they lagged or forgot a letter. Vasoula, the older child, was not allowed to transpose or skip letters or numbers, while Vangelis was given much more leeway, sometimes being allowed to recite letters (as well as poems and songs) in any order he pleased. At these times Eleni would comment to me "He's saying his own" (*Leei ta dika tou*). With Vasoula, on the other hand, Eleni did not allow regression. Having once reached a certain point of proficiency, Vasoula had to do at least that well each subsequent time.[9] Vangelis, being younger and not yet a regular school-attender, was allowed to practice in *psemata* frame, whereas Vasoula was held responsible for accuracy in *alitheia* frame.

---

[9]Bruner (1978) called this kind of prevention of slippage a *communicative ratchet*.

Memorizing TV Ads

A frequent activity between Kalliope and her younger brother Alexis was acting out advertisements seen on television. One in particular—an ad for *Soufflan,* a product for washing wool and other fine fabrics, similar to Woolite in the United States—was practiced over and over, so I recorded several occasions on video and audiotape. The ad consists of a husband and wife dialogue:

H. Where is my good pullover?
    (*Ma pou einai to kalo mou pulover;*)
W. In the wash
    (*Yia plisimo*)
H. My favorite pullover—I'll take it to the drycleaners!
    (*To agapimeno mou pulover—tha to pao kathiristirio*)
W. You'll see—with Soufflan, there's no worry—the dirt comes out easily without ruining the wool
    (*Tha dis—me to Soufflan, dhen ehei fovo—fevgei efkola i vromia horiz na katastrefei ta mallina*)

****

W. Well? (as husband tries on clean sweater)
    (*Lipon;*)
H. Mmm—like new
    (*Mmm—san kainouryio*)
W. The money (wife holds out hand)
    (*Ta lefta*)
H. What money?
    (*Pia lefta;*)
W. What you'd have given to the drycleaners!
    (*Pou tha'dones yia kathiristirio!*)

During their rehearsals of this dialogue and its accompanying gestures and actions, Kalliope would correct any errors on Alexis' part. Having practiced one round to Kalliope's satisfaction, they would then switch roles and do it over, so ultimately both children were able to carry on either side of the dialogue. Although the ad imitation is a kind of game and clearly not the same as the television model from which it is derived, the two children nonetheless operated in *alitheia* frame, Kalliope in particular insisting on correct performance by her little brother.

This brother and sister spontaneously chose to rehearse one TV ad to near perfection and others to a lesser degree. Why? They obviously enjoyed adding emphasis to the voices and gestures in much the same way that professional actors interpret a role. They also enjoyed trading roles. Kalliope made it clear that it was important to get the dialogue right, so while she encouraged gestural variations, she insisted on accuracy in speech. This begins to make sense when seen in the light of the many other opportunities for memorizing which Greek children have. Poems, stories, songs, the alphabet, and TV dialogues—all are part of a huge mass of information to be committed to memory. Children in the presence of adult audiences are often encouraged to perform by reciting a poem or singing a song. Children become proprietary about these texts, each child having one or several favorites; if another child begins to recite one of these same texts in front of an audience, the first child will begin to cry and protest, "I want to say it" (*Ego thelo na to po*), indicating that ownership of the text is critical.

CONCLUSION

In this chapter, we have looked at four examples of the *alitheia* frame (dancing, coffee-making, rehearsing a TV ad, and practicing literacy skills), and four examples of the *psemata* frame (cupping, rolling fillo, working in the fields, and practicing literacy skills). These examples suggest several possible functions for *psemata* framing in procedural teaching and learning.

First, the *psemata* frame can lead to a simplified process in which one or more components are omitted, as we saw in the cupping scene and in the younger child's literacy practice. In the literacy practice, components (letters of the alphabet) were not only omitted but also transposed and repeated. By simplifying or shaping the process, practice is made possible when it might otherwise be too difficult or dangerous.

Psemata framing can also be used to mark an activity that the learner does not have to learn, such as the *fillo* rolling. By framing Kalliope's participation in the task as fake, Katerina relieves the girl of any responsibility for learning. In this case, it is not that Kalliope is too young or the task too dangerous, but rather that the grandmother does not see it as a meaningful part of the girl's future. This stands in contrast to the scenes of cupping, working in the fields, and literacy practice, in which *psemata* framing functions as a place-holder for activities that will be taken on seriously when the learners are ready.

By teaching in *psemata* frame, teachers can adjust the task to the learner's level. In the literacy practice, the older child was held to *alitheia* performance, whereas the younger child was allowed to "say his own." He was encouraged to participate in whatever manner he could. Although the *psemata* frame in these examples encourages learner participation in tasks they might otherwise not try, it does not seem to move learners into the zone of proximal development. Rather, it enables them to practice or play at something without fear of failure or rigid correction routines. It allows them to "get the feel of things" without worrying about accurate performance.

6 Teaching and Learning to Understand

In the previous chapter, the dancing and cupping episodes illustrated how *alitheia* and *psemata* framing can influence interaction during procedural teaching and learning. This chapter focuses on *declarative* teaching and learning, in which the goal is to understand rather than to carry out a process. "Babyclothes," the first episode, is framed as *alitheia,* and "kinship," the second episode, is framed as *psemata*.

BABYCLOTHES

The teaching and learning episodes in the previous chapter involved processes that were for the most part traditional to Greek life. But certainly not all that is taught and learned in this community is traditional; people do bring new or modern ideas and technologies into the community, with varying degrees of acceptance. In the episode called "babyclothes," an experienced mother who lives most of the year in Athens introduces an inexperienced village mother to some relatively modern ideas and information about clothing for babies.

As background, readers need to know that traditional clothing for men, women, and children in Greece tends to be on the heavy side by most middle-class American standards, even with climatic differences taken into account. Elderly women in the village typically wear the traditional *karagouna* outfit consisting of a dark blue woolen dress with long sleeves, dark blue woolen socks or stockings, and some form of black rubber shoes for working in the wet earth. Elderly men wear old slacks, worn leather oxfords or rubber boots, woolen suit coats over long-sleeved shirts, and often woolen vests as well. Even in the hot, muggy summer months, when temperatures soar up to 40° C (or 104° F), the older generation dresses heavily. The middle generation wears lighter clothing consisting of cotton or synthetic dresses and plastic sandals without hose for women, and blue jeans and cotton shirts with plastic sandals or rubber boots for men. But in both generations a pronounced concern with catching cold (*krioma*) pervades. I was often warned, "You'll catch cold like that" (*Tha krioseis etsi*) when I wore what to me was normal, light clothing for very hot weather. If I sat on cement or marble steps, I was hastily given a mat or a blanket to intervene between me and the cement because "It is like a snake — it bites you" (*Einai san fidhi—se tsibaei*).

Because their own mothers or mothers-in-law are often the first and most available teachers, young mothers in the village tend to clothe their babies heavily in accordance with the attitudes of the older generation (and to some extent the middle one) toward cold. Changes in these practices come about through individuals who, having lived in urban settings, bring more modern attitudes and practices back to the village. It is in this context that the following vignette can best be understood.

Eleni's Lesson

There are six participants in this interaction:

Eleni, a 33-year-old village woman and first-time mother,
Soula, Eleni's cousin by marriage, also in her early 30s and mother of two boys; lives in Athens normally,
Maria, Eleni's mother,
Andreas, Soula's youngest son, age 6,
Bebis, Eleni's yet unbaptized 4-month-old son, and
Rosemary, the author.

It is June 17, 1986, a hot, humid afternoon in the village; Soula, her son Andreas, and I are visiting Eleni and her baby in Eleni's bedroom. Eleni's mother, Maria, is present some of the time. The baby is clothed heavily, perspiring, and making decidedly unhappy noises. Soula, the more experienced mother, advises Eleni to take off the heavy wool clothing her baby is wearing, pointing out that it is healthy for the baby to get a little air on his skin and to play unclothed for a while each day. Eleni removes all but the disposable diaper, and the baby begins to coo happily. However, Soula's reasoning does not impress Maria:

S. You see how—what he says now that he got a little air?
   (*Eides pos—ti leei tora pou pire ligo aera;*)
M. Of course, he wants it like that—but it's too bad though.
   (*Eh kala, thelei etsi— alla krima omos.*)
S. What's too bad? (*Ti krima;*)

. . . .

M. Aren't you going to put an undershirt on him?
   (*Dhen tha to val's siponaki;*)
E. I don't dress him in undershirts.
   (*Dhen to forao siponaki.*)
S. Leave him like that a little—let him play.
   (*As to etsi ligo—as to na paizei.*)
M. No no no no put it on!
   (*Ohi ohi ohi ohi val'to!*)

. . . .

S. Like this, Aunt, it's better.
   (*Etsi Theia einai pio kala.*)
M. Good for now, but what happens tomorrow?
   (*Kala tora, alla ti yinete avrio;*)

In this last question, Maria refers implicitly to the fear that the baby will catch cold. Soon after that, she leaves the room, and Eleni and Soula turn their full attention to a topic that was introduced a few turns back, the issue of how to deal with the problem of wetting. This leads to a very involved discussion about the different kinds of disposable diapers and underpants that are available. Soula gives Eleni advice about which to use in which situations. She points out that besides being more comfortable for the baby, it is more economical to let him play in cloth underpants part of the day "so as not to waste the Babylino (disposable diapers), which cost thirty drachmas each" (*na min halasei kai to Babylino, pou ehoun trianta dhrahmes to ena*). She tells Eleni to put a waterproof pad on the bed underneath him so that he doesn't get the mattress wet. She also tells her about a product for babies that resembles a sanitary napkin, and can be used inside a cloth panty to absorb wetness during the day. At night, she tells Eleni to use a disposable diaper. Eleni expresses confusion over the different brand names and terms: "I don't know, disposable diapers, I get them confused, my dear. . . ." (*Dhen xero, pana vrakaki, ta perdhevo re paidhi mou*). Soula explains to her that disposable diapers are available in several brands.

After this, the two women return to more general talk about the baby. Soula notes how much happier and more comfortable the baby is now:

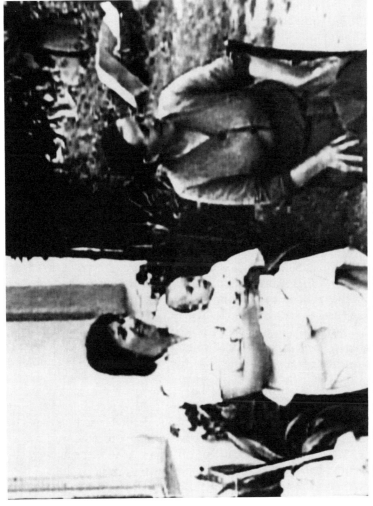

Figure 21. Eleni, her mother, and "Bebis" pose for the videocamera in front of their home.

S. He's good now; what does he want with the little shirt? And he doesn't wear the the cap that he wore in winter . . . and he put on summer-clothes and took off the undershirt.
(Kala einai aftos tora—ti zitaei me to poukamisaki—kai dhen foraei to ti kapa pou forouse to heimona . . . kai forese ta kalokairina kai evgale ti flanela)

E. He wears the light ones, the summer ones, eh Bebi?
(Foraei ap'afta ta lepta, ta kalokairina, eh Bebi?)

As Soula and Andreas start making motions to leave, Soula says, "More or less one can use oneself as an example; as you dress yourself, so should you try to dress the child. Since you're not cold, it means that the child won't get cold either" *(Ligo poli paradhigmatizetai o allos ap'ton eafto tou. Opos dinesai esi na prospathisei na dineis kai to paidhi as poume. Afou esi dhen krioneis paei na pi oti oute to paidhi tha krionei)*. At this point, the baby begins to whimper and Eleni asks him if he wants to eat. Soula directs Andreas to bring the baby's bottle, and shortly after that they get up and leave.[1]

Interpretation

Initiation. The initiating moment of this episode occurred before I turned the tape recorder on. Eleni had been confiding in me about some personal matters before Soula and her son entered, so I had taken care not to record anything. Shortly after Soula entered and sat down on the bed, she initiated the teaching by pointing out that the baby was overdressed and by directing Eleni to take off his clothes. Her initiation was clearly contextualized by the obvious discomfort of the baby, who in his unhappy state presented a problem that wanted resolution. Soula apparently took this as a cue to teach Eleni something from her own experience in childrearing.

Task Structure. In describing task structure, we encounter one of the differences between procedural and declarative teaching. Activities like dancing and cupping consist of separate and definable actions that a teacher may verbalize through separate directives and link together to form a set of actions. Together, these actions constitute the goal of the activity. But the discussion in babyclothes is not about steps to take in clothing a baby and does not have definable units of action, nor is a set of actions the goal here. This is a different kind of teaching in which a knowledge system, rather than a set of actions, is the basis of the teaching. Participants communicate the knowledge system primarily through talk, and thus it is the talk that reveals structural elements.

---

[1]The full transcript of this episode appears in Appendix E.

One of the most useful tools of discourse analysis, particularly when studying the structure of a large stretch of discourse, is topic analysis. By looking at what is being talked about, who introduces topics, and in what sequence they are introduced, we can gain an overall picture of the organization of talk and see more clearly how topics are related to one another. Most of the topics addressed in this episode (except the tape recorder topic) center on the baby. The topics appear in order of occurrence below, with a star indicating topics that are "inserted" within a more continuous topic. Of the 22 topics that occur in the transcript, 13 involve teaching and learning; these are indicated with bold letters.[2]

1. tape recorder
2. Andreas talking to baby*
3. tape recorder
4. **baby getting air**
5. **waterproof pad**
6. **undershirt (*ziponaki*)**
7. **underpants**
8. **different brands of diapers (Babylino & Pampers)**
9. **baby getting air**
10. Andreas talking to baby
11. where Andreas went
    (gap in transcript; Eleni talks to Andreas here)
12. **baby's happy sounds**
13. **what to put on baby's feet**
14. what baby's father will say
15. **summer clothes (get rid of winter ones)**
16. baby trying to take off diaper
17. **fooling baby with pacifier**
18. **baby sweating/heat at night**
19. **general rule for clothing baby***
20. **heat at night**
21. giving baby bottle
22. Soula and Andreas leaving

From this we see the extent to which teaching and learning permeate the overall talk. Of the 13 topics that involve some teaching and/or learning,

---

[2]Discourse analysts have proposed a number of ways of determining discourse topics in an effort to make the notion less intuitive and more precise. In this analysis I approximated procedures outlined by Givon (1983), looking at topic continuity (the use of pronouns to continue referring to already established nouns, and other markers of new versus given information). Also, following Brown and Yule (1983) I took into account paratones, pauses, and speaker change.

Soula initiates 8, Eleni 4 (2 of which are re-entries of topics Soula had
brought up earlier), and Maria 1. In this analysis, initiation is conceived as
simply the first mention of a topic, or first mention after other topics have
intervened (see Table 4).

These lists of topics and initiations provide evidence for the intuitive
judgements that teaching and learning are primary activities here, and that
Soula controls much of this instruction by virtue of her more frequent
initiations. When Eleni initiates, she initiates as a learner, engaging Soula in
forming a response. The topic list also reveals the content of the teaching,
which can be summarized as follows:

Knowledge about babyclothes:
- Which clothes to leave off in hot weather
- What to do if/when baby wets
- What kind of protection to use (underpants, pad, diapers, plastic
  pants)
- What brands of diaper exist and what they make
- Whether to give baby pacifier

With the exception of the pacifier segment,[3] the content areas of teaching
are closely related. Taken together, they form a knowledge system in which
the parts are related both to one another and to the superordinate topic,
knowledge about babyclothes. Parts are related in two primary ways: First,
there is the general-to-specific relationship between giving the baby some air
and discussing which particular clothes to leave off; second, there is the
relationship of action to possible consequences, exemplified by the concern
that the unclothed baby might wet the bed; finally, there is again a
general-to-specific relationship between preventing the baby from wetting
the bed and the specific means of prevention, including the discussion of
diaper brands. Thus, the parts are related to one another and to the
superordinate topic through a set of logical links. In some cases, participants express these links overtly through connectives such as the following:

". . . **if** you don't want him to get wet . . . "
(. . . *a'ma the's na mi mouskevei* . . .)
        and
"underpants only **so that he won't** waste the Babylino which cost thirty
drachmas each."
(*vrakaki mono **na min** halasei kai ta Babylino pou ehoun trianta
dhrahmes to ena*)

---

[3]The topic of the pacifier was taken up because Eleni gave the baby a pacifier at that moment
and commented that "he doesn't always take it," thereby providing an opportunity for Soula
to teach about the use of pacifiers.

TABLE 4
Topics in Babyclothes Episode

Soula	Eleni	Maria
Getting air	Waterproof panties	Undershirt
Waterproof pad	Something for feet	
Diaper brands	Pacifier	
Getting air	Heat at night	
Happy sounds		
Summer clothing		
Sweating		
General rule		

These links recall the traditional rhetorical modes used in teaching expository writing and speaking. Exposition, as it has traditionally been taught, consists of a thesis or main argument and a body of related information that develops and supports the thesis. The development might include reasons why one should believe the thesis, specific instances or examples of the thesis (which could include narrative to illustrate a point), counterarguments, consequences of the thesis, and other logical connections. Expository discourse is usually contrasted with narrative discourse, in which parts are related either through chronological order (or some transformation thereof) or through space (e.g., a description of a place).

The Soviet model used in the previous chapter to depict the different levels of activity served adequately to show not only the structure of the task, but also which subtasks were being taught in a given situation. Applying this same model to an instance of declarative teaching, however, one finds that it fails to discriminate among the different types of logical connections. Discussing how to deal with the consequences of "giving baby some air" is very different from telling a child to "use the worry beads too" as part of a dance. The model is good at representing instruction that foregrounds parts of a process because it needs only to show the hierarchical relationship of parts (subtasks) to wholes or larger parts. However, it is much more complicated to represent instruction in knowledge systems such as babyclothes because subcomponents like "what clothes to leave off" and "what to do about wetting" are related differently to the superordinate topic. The first elaborates on the general notion of making the baby more comfortable, while the second presents a solution to one of the consequences of leaving clothing off.

Instructional Interaction.   The role of teacher is taken up at various points by Soula, Maria, and Andreas. Maria's attempts to teach, described in the vignette, are shortlived, probably due to the conflict between her views and Soula's. Soula gains ascendancy as a teacher when Maria leaves the room. Andreas makes only one attempt to teach (or more accurately, to imitate teaching discourse), when he says, "I say you should put thin socks on him" (*Ego leo na ton valeis leptes kaltses*). In the next utterance, Eleni repeats his utterance twice, laughing between repetitions and thus communicating to Andreas that the role of teacher is inappropriate for him. Thus, Soula remains, throughout most of the interaction, the predominant teacher.

Soula communicates her intent to teach in a number of direct ways. Following are some of the utterances that illustrate this intention:

1. **You should have it** [waterproof pad] here.
   (*Na toh's edo pera*)
2. **Leave him** like that [unclothed] a little; **let him** play.
   (*As to etsi ligo. As to na paizei*)
3. **Let him be** dear to get some air, the child.
   (*As ton mari na parei aera to paidhi*)
4. **Like this** [without undershirt], Aunt, **it's better.**
   (*Etsi, Theia, einai pio kala*)
5. Yes, **you should put** on his panties only; **don't put** on Babylino; **leave him** like this to play.
   (*Nai, na to vazeis vraki mono. Na mi to vazei Babylino. Na t'afins etsi na paixei*)
6. A cloth diaper only, **so you won't** waste the Babylino which cost thirty drachmas each.
   (*Vrakaki mono, **na min** halasei kai to Bebilino pou ehoun trianta dhrahmes to ena*)
7. Yes, **you'll put** that [diaper] as we put ours [sanitary pad] and you'll put the panties over it.
   (*Nai, **tha to vazei** ekeino opos vazoume emeis kai tha vazeis kai to kilotaki apo pano*)
8. Of course at night if you don't want him to get wet . . . **it's better to** use this [waterproof diaper—Pampers etc.] rather than that [cloth diaper & panties] but for the day that [cloth] must be cheaper, more economical.
   (*Kala ti nihta vevaia ama the's na mi mouskevei, na mi ftiahnei, **einai pio kala** afto para ekeino, alla etsi yia ti mera ekeino prepei na einai pio fthino, pio ikonomiko*)
9. **Better not to**—I—they [my children] never took those [pacifiers] they didn't use them even if I forced them to . . .
   (***Kalitera min** tin—ego—dhen piran pote afta, dhen tin epairnan me to zori . . .*)
10. More or less one can use oneself as an example; as you dress yourself, **so should you try to dress** the child . . . since you're not cold it means that the child won't get cold either.

(*Ligo poli paradhigmatizetai o allos ap'ton eafto tou. Opos dinesai esi **na prospathisei na dineis** kai to paidhi as poume. Afou esi dhen krioneis paei na pi oti oute to paidhi tha krionei*)

The teaching of declarative knowledge usually requires some contextualization, especially in the form of reasons. In the babyclothes episode Soula provides a number of reasons for her teaching. She appeals frequently to the baby's happier state now that his heavy clothing is off, referring to his contented cooing, getting air on his legs, and moving his legs more freely; she states in general "Like this, Aunt, it's better." Later, when the topic shifts to the different kinds of protection, Soula points out that economy is a factor too; Eleni will save money by not using the plastic Babylino diapers all the time.

Another way of contextualizing is to compare the unfamiliar, new information to something more familiar. Soula does this in two instances. First she compares the product that goes inside the underpants to sanitary napkins and later she generalizes that the rule of thumb is to use one's own comfort as a guide to the baby's comfort.

Soula also contextualizes her teaching in a third way by taking on the voice and perspective of the baby. She does this both directly and indirectly. In the direct form, she simulates a "baby-like" voice (higher pitch, etc) to speak directly as baby to the mother, Eleni:

"Make me, Mama," say, "to get a little air on my legs."
(*Kane me, Mama, pes, na paro ligo aerako sta podharakia*)
"You suffocated me, Mama," tell her, "you put both blankets over me . . . the winter ones, and you made me wear the heavy jumpsuits, too."
(*M'eskases re Mama, pes, m'evales kai tis dio tis kouvertes . . . tis himoniatikes . . . m'evales kai tis hondres tis formes*)

By assuming the baby's voice, Soula again provides reasons for her teaching, only this time they are framed not as her reasons but rather the baby's. Because all of this is presumeably for the sake of the baby, it is important that he have a voice, or, as he can't yet speak, a slot for his voice.

Soula also assumes the perspective of the baby indirectly by interpreting the baby's feelings and needs in the third person. For example:

"You see what he says now that he got a little air?"
(*Eidhes ti lei tora pou pire aera ligo;*)
"He's happy, eh? He's all gladness."
(*Hairete eh; olo hares einai*)

"He's good now; what does he want with the little shirt, and he doesn't wear the cap that he wore in winter . . . he put on his summer clothes and took off the undershirt."

(*Kala einai aftos, ti zitaei me to poukamisaki kai dhen foraei to ti kapa pou forouse to heimona . . . kai forese ta kalokairina kai evgale ti flanela*)

In light of these interpretations, both direct and indirect, it is interesting to note that Soula contradicts herself (or at least contradicts her deeds) at the end of the episode. Just as she prepares to state the general rule of thumb, she hedges by saying, "We might say . . .who knows what the child wants? But more or less one can use oneself as an example." She didn't hesitate to interpret what the child felt and wanted earlier; why should she do so now? Her hedging may be related to the generality of the statement that follows. Although it is acceptable to interpret what a baby wants in a specific instance, it is another thing entirely to generalize across instances and state a rule of thumb. She may be using the hedge to soften the impact of such a generalization.

Soula's rule of thumb adds a note of formality in so far as closing generalizations such as this are more common in formal schooling. This may be another key to understanding why she hedges here; she is treading on more formal territory than the rest of the episode warranted. She is also invoking considerable authority by claiming to know not only how this baby wants to be clothed now, but how all babies want to be clothed in any given circumstances. By taking on such authority, she has the potential to threaten Eleni's face—Eleni who, until now, has been only slightly less knowledgeable than Soula. Softening her authority with the hedge is one way of maintaining a peer relationship with Eleni.

Eleni indicates her intent to learn in a number of instances, as the examples here show:

1. You're right; I haven't put anything but Pampers on him, never panties. (acknowledging other's expertise)
   (*Kala les, ego dhen ton eho foresei katholou ektos apo Pampers, pote kilotaki*)
2. But that—with what—it's inside the panties, eh? (asking for information)
   (*Alla ekeinone, ti einai, mesa se kilotaki eh;*)
3. I see. (indicating grasp of new information)
   (*Katalava*)
4. That's Babylino which is like a sanitary napkin. (checking to confirm understanding)
   (*Ekeino einai Bebilino pou einai sa servieta*)

5. I don't know—disposable diapers—I get them confused, my dear (stating confusion)
   (*Dhen xero, pana vrakaki, ta perdhevo re paidhi mou*)
6. I didn't know that. (stating ignorance)
   (*Dhen to'xera*)

The baby himself provides the most overt evaluation of the success of the new method. His cooings and other happy noises are evidence that the undressing was a good idea. Even Maria has to acknowledge that the baby is happier this way, for the present. His positive reactions are used by Soula to add evidence to her case.

There is no overt evaluation of Eleni's learning, however, nor is it called for; Eleni hasn't "done" anything that Soula could evaluate. Eleni has been learning, but not practicing or performing any aspect of what she has learned. Her learning is indicated in statements like those above. When she says, "I didn't know that" (that Babylino, as well as other companies, makes plastic pants) she implies that she does know it now. "I see" (referring to Soula's advice to combine a cheap pad with cloth underpants for daytime) also indicates understanding. Even stronger evidence of learning, of course, would lie in Eleni's behavior on subsequent days; however, I did not observe consistently enough to see whether she dressed the baby more lightly. Also, one cannot forget that Eleni has other factors to contend with besides Soula's advice. She lives with her mother, and her mother has made it clear that she dissapproves of Soula's way of dressing the baby. Thus, even though Eleni has learned from Soula, she may refrain from changing her behavior in order to avoid conflict with her mother.

Relationship Between Learner's Zone of Proximal Development and Teaching. Eleni indicates through her talk that some of the knowledge system Soula delineates is new to her. Direct evidence of this newness can be seen in utterances where she expresses confusion ("I don't know—disposable diapers—I get them confused my dear") or past ignorance ("I didn't know that"). Through Soula's intervention as a teacher, Eleni is exposed to newness on many different levels. She hears that babies do not necessarily have to be heavily clothed at all times and that playing unclothed sometimes may be good for them; she hears of products she had not known of, and she revises her understanding of brand names, the products they make, and their uses.

Soula, for her part, uses strategies of teaching that may make it easier for Eleni to absorb the new information. She motivates her by pointing out how much happier the baby seems, relates the unfamiliar to the familiar, and provides a generalization at the end, but she does not simplify the knowledge system itself. That is, she tries her best to communicate effectively about the system, but this does not entail omission or transformation of any of the major components of the system as she knows it. In this sense, the overall character of the instruction resembles scaffolding more than shaping.

KINSHIP

Children everywhere learn about the kinship system that surrounds and supports them. They acquire this knowledge in a number of ways, one of which is through the forms of address that they hear used, such as *Mama*, *Baba* (Daddy), *Xadelfe* (Cousin), *Theie* (Uncle), and so on. These terms provide a key to the child's emerging schema of who's who and what constitutes the relationships. However these terms can at the same time be confusing, for adults are not consistent in their ways of addressing one another. The terms can variously represent a blood relationship, a relationship through marriage, and a symbolic relationship.

Throughout my stay in Kiriakitsa I was treated as kin and expected to behave as such. Thus, Katerina and Grigoris often referred to me as a daughter or daughter-in-law, and I called them *Mama* and *Baba,* which was their wish. This must have been confusing to Alexis, who had never seen me before I appeared one day in April 1986 and suddenly became an integral part of the family. In the following vignette, he tries to resolve this confusion, but then stumbles into other confusing areas of kinship. Katerina, in *psemata* frame, refrains from clarifying the difference between blood and symbolic kinship, but Alexis does not know this.

Whose Mama?

It is the morning of June 9, 1986; Alexis is playing with some of his toy vehicles on the kitchen floor at his grandparents' house in the village. Katerina, his grandmother, is embroidering and I am reading nearby. In the middle of his playing, which involves invented dialogues between various drivers, Alexis addresses us and asks, "Did it [one of his vehicles] move by itself?" (*Mono tou pohorise?*). Katerina and I offer differing opinions about this, and suddenly Katerina realizes that Alexis' question is recalled from some earlier event that she assumed he had forgotten. She is surprised at his powerful memory and wonders, "Will you remember the letters too, or will you be like your sister, you'll forget them?" (*Tha thimase kai ta grammata,*[4] *i tha eisai san tin adhelfoula s' tha ta xehnas?*).

---

[4]The word *grammata* literally means letters (both alphabet and correspondance), but is often used as a shorthand to refer to a broad range of knowledge acquired in school, especially literacy and numeracy, as well as higher level use of these skills.

Although I have not addressed Katerina as Mama in this stretch of dialogue, Alexis nonetheless asks me shortly after, "Why do you call her Mama?" (*Yiati esi tin les Mama;*) Katerina takes charge of answering in a series of responses that continually throw the questions back at Alexis, for example,

K. Doesn't she have me as mama?
   (*Mama dhen m'ehei;*)
A. Yes, why are you a mama?
   (*Nai, yiati eisai mama;*)
K. I'm a mama, aren't I a mama?
   (*Eimai mama, dhen eimai mama;*)

Alexis changes tactics then, switching to a different relationship, that of his mother to Katerina. Here, however, a misunderstanding occurs:

A. My own mama?
   (*I giki mou i mama;*) [5]
K. Your Kiki, doesn't she have a mother?
   (*I Kiki sou dhen ehei mama?*)
A. She calls you 'Mama' too [6]
   (*Kai sena se leei kai Mama*)
K. Kiki calls me Grandma, how should she say; she has Nina as mama.
   (*I Kiki me leei Yiayia, pos na pi, Mama ehei ti Nina.*)

After this interchange, Alexis changes tactics again, this time constructing a question that asks about the relationship between Rosy and his mother:

A. "What does Rosy call my mama?"
   (*I Rosy pos ti leei ti mama mou;*)
K. Nina
A. How?
   (*Pos yia;*)
K. How should she call her?
   (*Pos na tin pi;*)
A. She should call her grandma
   (*Na, na ti leei yiayia*)

---

[5]*Giki mou* is a mispronunciation of *dhiki mou,* which means "my own." Katerina hears *Kiki mou* which means "my Kiki." Kiki is Alexis' sister's nickname.
[6]"She" here refers to Nina, A's mother.

K. Is your mother a grandma? Hey Alexi, why do you mix it up for us?
   (*Yiayia einai i mana sou; re Alexi, yiati mas ta perdheveis;*)

Finally I intervene with a generalization, explaining that to be a grandma, your children must have children of their own. Alexis says he understands, and then returns to his play with trucks.[7]

Interpretation

Initiation. Alexis initiates this teaching and learning episode by asking the question, "Why do you call her 'Mama'?" (*Yiati esi ti les "Mama";*). This question asks for understanding, for a reason *why*. Thus, we know, even at this early point, that the teaching and learning here will be more declarative than procedural. We also can assume that Alexis will have a vested interest in learning because he initiated the episode.

The *psemata* frame, on the other hand, is initiated and controlled by Katerina. She responds to Alexi's question by asking another question: "Doesn't she have me as mama?" (*Mama dhen m'ehei;*) The question as response to a question has an interesting effect, for it challenges Alexis to seek further for the answer, and at the same time it conceals from him some of the information he would need to answer the question correctly. Katerina implies that she is my mother in the biological sense, which is not true. Alexis, however, is not made party to the frame. Goffman (1974) called this type of frame a "benign fabrication." A fabrication in Goffman's terminology is a frame in which one or more individuals intentionally manage an activity so that others will not know of the frame.[8] A benign fabrication is one "engineered in the interest of the person contained" or at least not done against his interest. Among the various types of benign fabrications, Goffman listed "training hoaxes" in which "The neophyte is treated as though he were engaged in the real thing, and only later is he let in on the secret that all along his activity was occuring in protective insulation from the world he thought he had in view" (p. 96). This description, although it refers to an activity rather than a knowledge system, reflects the benign withholding of information we see in this episode.

Katerina uses a teasing style that makes the question different from a straightforward information question. She knows the answer, or at least has an opinion; she also knows that the listener does not have enough information to answer the question fully, yet will try anyway. Rather than seeking information, the question is an attempt to get the learner to reveal his state of knowledge. This style of questioning is brought up again in a later example in this chapter.

---

[7]The transcript of this episode appears in Appendix E.

[8]Fabrication is contrasted to *keying* in so far as keying involves mutual establishment of a frame by all participants (i.e., all agree that "this is play").

Task Structure and Transformation.   Katerina and Alexis have some-what different goals in this interaction. They talk at cross purposes several times, and Katerina does not address his questions directly. The fact that Katerina and Alexis have different goals leads them to see the task and the structure of the task differently.

Katerina's goal is to help Alexis sort out the labels used in addressing and referring to kin. Alexis' goal is to know why someone is called a mother. He wants an explanation; she wants him to induce the correct labels through her questioning.

One can think of kinship as a vast system of relationships, including all the variations based on blood, marriage, and symbolic bonds, as well as the different points of view that must be understood in order to talk about kinship apart from one's own central position. Alexis thinks that because Katerina is *Yiayia* to him, she is *Yiayia* to everyone. Katerina and other adults, on the other hand, have long ago internalized this rather abstract system; to a large extent within a given community, members share the same cognitive model of kinship. Alexis is asking for information about this adult model. Although Katerina controls the information, Alexis controls the forward movement of the conversation, for he is the one who initiates topic changes. His topics are listed here:

1. Why is Katerina a mama?
2. Why does Alexis' mother call Katerina "Mama"?
3. What does RH call Alexis' mother?

What Alexis asks for, then, is an explanation of at least the aspects of kinship surrounding the notion of "mother." What he receives, through Katerina's benign fabrication, is a simplified version, a shaping of the adult model. He is not told, for instance, that Nina and I call Katerina "Mama" for different reasons.

This information constitutes a system of knowledge, as did the babyclothes information structure. Both are taught and learned declaratively rather than procedurally. Talk constitutes the main mode of instruction, and through talk a system of relationships is explored.

Instructional Interaction.   This interaction differs from others we have examined in that teaching is not carried out through directives and modeling as we saw in the procedural examples, nor through the kind of elaborate explanations we saw in the babyclothes episode. Instead, Katerina carries out the teacher's role mainly through questioning.

Alexis also questions almost continually. As noted earlier, his questions are the ones that move the interaction forward through several topic shifts that he initiates. Indeed, Alexis is an extremely active and persistent learner here, and despite Katerina's benign fabrication, he continues to try to make some sense of the kinship system. He illustrates rather well the phrase often used in educational circles, "taking charge of his/her own learning." His question about why I call Katerina "Mama" and the reformulation of that question into "Why are you a mama" are especially persistent, appearing four times altogether.

Katerina, for her part, contributes to Alexis' active role. By providing little new information and by asking many questions, she provides a context in which Alexis must clarify what it is he wants to know. Her questions also serve to draw out the child's understanding, as the following example shows:

> K. I'm a mama, aren't I a mama?
> (*Eimai mama, dhen eimai mama;*)
> A. No
> (*Ohi*)
> K. What am I?
> (*Ti eimai?*)
> A. You're a grandma.
> (*Yiayia eisai*)

Katerina uses the question, "What am I?" to pinpoint Alexis' view of the system. His response makes it clear that he has not yet acquired the notion of kinship other than in relation to himself.

The presence of a number of linguistic features indicating a point of view other than the self suggest that one of the main things Alexis is learning here is really "How to think about kinship from the standpoint of others." These features include:

> 1. Asking "What does X call Y?"
> 2. Saying "X has Y as ____"
> 3. Saying "I am a ____ for you."
> 4. Saying "For X, Y is a ____"

Several of Alexis' utterances provide proximal indicators of learning. He apparently understands that there is something about other people's points of view that makes the kinship terms change from person to person. The following exchange illustrates his evolving awareness that his grandma may bear a different relationship to other people, such as myself:

> K. What am I? (*Ti eimai;*)
> A. You're a grandma (*Yiayia eisai*)
> K. I'm a Grandma for *you* (*Yiayia eimai yia sena*)
> A. For Rosy? (*Yia ti Rosy;*)

In the following exchange, he pursues this concept of decentralization further, aware that although he calls his mother "mama," I might call her something different:

A. Rosy, how does she call my mama?
   (*I Rosy pos ti leei ti mama mou?*)
K. Ni Nina
A. How (*Pos yia*)
K. How should she call her? (*Pos na ti pi?*)
A. She should call her grandma (*Na na ti leei yiayia*)

Obviously his view of kinship does not yet match the adult model. He may be trying out a hypothesis wherein reversal is the controlling pattern; that is, if Rosy calls his grandma "Mama," then maybe she calls his mother "Grandma." The fact that his concept does not yet match the adult concept does not mean, however, that he has learned nothing in this exchange. He has acquired the relevant questions to ask in order to make sense of the system and has figured out that the meaningful distinction is the question "For whom?"

At the end of the transcript, after my generalization about what makes people grandmas, Alexis says "Yes I understood, and I also will become . . ." (*Nai katalava, kai 'go sa yino . . .*) . This too can be seen as a proximal indicator of learning. However, caution should be exercised in inferring what people mean when they say, "I understand" or "I see." People often say these things to move the conversation along, to indicate that they are listening, or to show politeness, whether or not they have understood. And if they have understood, the surrounding discourse may provide clues as to what that was. "I understand" can refer to the immediately preceding proposition of the other speaker, or it can refer to a whole prior text. In the case of Alexis, we can only rely on his next phrase, "and I also will become" (*kai 'go sa yino*) to tell us what he understood. He seems to be referring strictly to the preceding utterances about what makes people grandparents. After that, he moves back to his toy cars, and the topic of kinship is closed.

In the process of trying to understand kinship, Alexis also gains practice and help in developing his communicative skills, particularly those related to the development of a fuller syntax that includes all the necessary information about actors and actions, as the following example shows:

A. The the the my mama how
   (*Ti ti ti mama mou pos*)
K. Your mama
   (*Ti mama sou*)

A. The the my mama how does s/he call her my mama how?
   (*Ti ti mama mou pos ti leei ti mama mou pos?*)
K. Who?
   (*Pios?*)
A. What does Rosy call my mama?
   (*I Rosy pos ti leei ti mama mou;*)

Here Alexis' discourse is being "scaffolded" by Katerina in a way very similar to descriptions by Bruner (1978), and others. Through her questions, she extends his communicative ability until he is able to ask the complete question with all its nouns and pronouns marked correctly for case. Thus, as with so many teaching and learning interactions both in and out of school, there is more than one thing being learned.

Relation Between Learner's Zone of Proximal Development and Teaching.   Alexis' zone of proximal development in this episode is evidently at a point where notions of kinship are being stretched to include not only other people's relationships to him as the center but also other people's relationships to each other. These relationships of others to others are the difficult part, the part that he doesn't quite understand yet.

Through the *psemata* frame Katerina withholds certain information that might complicate the matter too much. She is able thus to concentrate more fully on the "problem" as Alexis sees it. In a sense then, this episode involves both scaffolding and shaping. Katerina shapes the kinship system by transforming it to a simplified version; she scaffolds it by using questions to provide dialogic support and to enable Alexis to see where his understanding was unlike the adult model.

COMPARISON

The babyclothes and kinship episodes differ from the cupping and dancing episodes in that they involve the teaching and learning of knowledge systems rather than sets of meaningful action. They are taught declaratively with focus on the relationships among elements in the knowledge system. Furthermore, the primary mode of communication in these episodes is talk. Thus, the structure of the knowledge system as it is taught is to be found primarily in the ways people organize their talk around topics or other types of contrast in talk. At the end of each episode there is a generalization about the subject matter; Soula provides it in babyclothes, and I provide it in kinship.

Both episodes involve some conflict. In babyclothes, it is conflict between Maria and Soula about the way the baby should be clothed. This can be seen in a larger context as a conflict of traditional versus modern attitudes

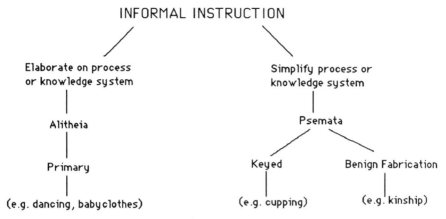

Figure 22.   Interpretive frames: three instructional options.

toward cold. In kinship, the conflict is more subtle, involving the difference in Alexis' and Katerina's concept of the task. Alexis wants an explanation, whereas Katerina takes her task as helping him find the right labels for people.

There are several differences between the two episodes. Although both take place within a social context that involves familiars, the babyclothes episode involves greater social distance between the participants. And certainly, the age of the participants in the babyclothes episode sets it apart from other episodes in these chapters. Another difference is that in babyclothes, the teaching/learning is initiated by the teacher (with clear contextual cues from the baby), whereas in kinship, it is initiated by the learner.

The main difference, however, lies in the way the knowledge system is handled by the teacher. In babyclothes, Soula elaborates on the system in great detail, making no attempt to transform or simplify the system itself as she conceives it, although she does use teaching strategies such as relating the strange to the familiar in order to make the content more accessible to Eleni. In kinship, on the other hand, Katerina greatly simplifies the knowledge system but does not call attention to this through any overt framing, in contrast to the cupping episode in which the teacher framed the episode clearly as *psemata*. For this reason, the simplification remains in Goffman's terms a *benign fabrication* in which Alexis is "contained."

We have now seen three framing possibilities in operation—primary, keyed, and benignly fabricated. Figure 22 illustrates these options.

OTHER DECLARATIVE TEACHING AND LEARNING

Several other declarative episodes provide further contextualization of this mode of teaching and learning.

Expressing Emotion

On two occasions I observed Alexis being taught about a different kind of knowledge system, the system of emotions and appropriate ways of expressing them. The following exerpts from my fieldnotes describe the two situations:

1. After lunch, silence descends as everyone lies down or reads, or does some sort of quiet activity. Outside my window, 22-year-old Tonis is attending to the finer details of car clean-up when Alexis joins him. The following interaction takes place, quietly, under my window:

Tonis, in the context of a larger conversation that I didn't overhear, tells Alexis he loves him.

A. Why do you say it?
   (*Yiati to les;*)
T. Why shouldn't I say it?
   (*Yiati na min to po;*)
A. Since I know it
   (*Afou to xero*)
T. How do you know it?
   (*Pos to xereis;*)
A. I just know it
   (*Etsi, to xero*)
T. And because you know it, does that mean I shouldn't say it? I like to say it.
   (*Kai afou to xereis prepei na min to po; Emena m'aresei na to po.*)
A. OK
   (*Endaxi*)
T. Do you like to hear it?
   (*S'aresei na to akous;*)
A. Yes, I like it
   (*Nai, m'aresei.*)
T. Do you love me?
   (*Emena m'agapas;*)
A. What do you think, don't I love you?
   (*Em ti, dhen s'agapo;*)
T. You know, it's not nice to say "em ti." Say, "Yes, I love you."
   (*Xereis, dhen einai oraio na peis "em ti." Pes "Nai, s'agapo."*)
A. And why is it not nice?
   (*Kai yiati dhen einai oraio;*)
T. It just doesn't sound good.
   (*Etsi, dhen akouyete kala*)

At this point Katerina appears and tries to get Alexis to come in and lie down and stop bothering Tonis. Tonis intervenes, saying, "No, it's OK, we're talking" (*Ohi, einai endaxi; emeis milame*).

Katerina leaves again. Alexis and Tonis go on talking a bit, then fall silent, and then both begin quietly singing the *Frango Siriani,* one of Alexis' favorite songs.

2. Thomas, Alexis' father, has just told Alexis to take off his sweater because the child is perspiring from dancing. Alexis refuses. Thomas then places his open palm next to Alexis' face — a threatening gesture — and says, "Will you take it off?" (*Tha to vgaleis;*).

"Yes," replies Alexis, undoing his buttons and removing the sweater.

A couple of minutes later, Alexis, sobbing, asks his father, "Why did you do that with your hand?" (*Yiati m'ekanes etsi me to heri;*).

Thomas replies that it was because Alexis didn't listen to words alone. He continues to explain, but Alexis interrupts and says, "Leave me alone, I'm angry" (*Ase me, eho nevra*). He repeats this several times until his father stops talking to him.

A few more minutes ensue, during which Thomas talks with his daughter and me. Then Thomas turns to Alexis again, who is now playing with toy cars under a table, and asks, "Are we friends now?" (*Eimaste filoi tora;*).

Alexis doesn't answer. Thomas asks again: "Tell me, are we friends again? I want to hear it" (*Pes, eimaste filoi pali; Thelo na to akouow*).

"Yes," (*Nai*) says Alexis.

Thomas asks Alexis if he will obey next time he tells him to do something.

"No" (*Ohi*), replies Alexis.

"No!" (*Ohi!*) — Thomas acts surprised and asks his son, "If you tell me to do something, do I have to do it?" (*An mou les emena na kano kati, prepei na to kano;*)

"Yes" (*Nai*), says Alexis.

"Ah, in other words, you don't have to do what I say, but I have to do what you say?" (*Ah dhiladhi dhen einai anangi na kaneis oti leo ego, alla ego prepei na kano oti les esi;*)

"Yes" (*Nai*), repeats Alexis.

"I'm little and you're big" (*Ego eimai mikros kai 'si eisai megalos*), says Thomas.

"Yes" (*Nai*), says Alexis.

These two scenes are noteworthy in several respects. Both teachers convey a message about the expression of emotion, that it is not enough to just feel certain feelings (e.g., love, friendship); one should also express them to the people for whom one has these feelings. Both are scenes of declarative teaching in that Alexis is not being taught *how* to do something as a process, but rather *about* feelings and their expression. A system of emotional connections is being exposed for him to understand. The participants take this teaching very seriously; no one is kidding or playing or in any way marking these scenes as anything other than *alitheia*. The fact that in both cases it is older male role models who are doing the emotional teaching toward a young boy makes these scenes interesting in terms of gender. At the least, these scenes contrast with the stereotype in the United States that men are not expected to express their emotions as much as women. And finally, the aftermath of emotional teaching is worth noting: The first scene ends with Tonis and Alexis singing a song together and the second ends with Thomas and Alexis role playing each other. In both cases, equality and sharing are stressed, and the tension of the previous emotional issues (Do you love me? Are we friends?) is resolved.

Radiation

The Chernobyl nuclear accident, which occurred in the Soviet Union in May 1986 and sent radiation throughout Europe, was an occasion for a great deal of declarative teaching and learning among Greeks of all social and economic classes. Television and radio reports informed us a day or two after the fact that Greece too had high levels of radiation, and advised us about precautions to take (e.g., not to drink fresh milk or eat the meat of free-grazing animals, not to eat leafy vegetables, not to go swimming in open waters, etc.). However, the information was sketchy, leaving much to the imagination. Many villagers thought of radiation as a fine powder that, once rinsed off, was gone. The fact that it goes into the soil and water systems and continues to be active for many years was difficult for them to imagine. Everyone had some information, but no one had a lot, so many heated discussions took place in which information was shared and disputed, but participants still went away with unsatisfactory answers. There simply were no experts in the immediate social environment.

Mothers and grandmothers were in a particularly tenuous position because they were the ones who decided, under normal circumstances, what the family would eat. They were also, being typically the least educated and the most restricted in their social networks, least likely to know what was safe and what was not. Aside from television, which anyone could watch (but not everybody could understand, if the program assumed schooling as background), information was disseminated mainly by men to women and other men. At a public lecture that I attended in Trikala on the subject of radiation and the Chernobyl accident, approximately 60% of the audience consisted of men over the age of 50, with little representation of women and young people.

One of the problems with all of the information that was disseminated through the media and public lectures was that it remained abstract, failing to address the specific, day-to-day decisions that had to be made: Could one or could one not drink chamomile tea made from chamomile that grew wild in the fields, provided one washed it thoroughly? The media had not said one could not eat chicken eggs, but did they assume that chickens were kept in sheds, unlike the village chickens that foraged freely outside? These were the kind of questions that plagued villagers, and no one seemed to know the answers, although many offered their opinions. This was an example of a crisis time in which insider networks could not provide experts equal to the task of educating their members. Information and teaching had to come from considerably beyond the inner circle, and transmission proved difficult and extremely uneven. Most people erred on the conservative side and chose to eat only dried legumes and macaroni for a month or more, to be safe. Only old people were cavalier, eating fresh vegetables or drinking chamomile and saying, "I'll be dead in a few years anyway."

Exam Preparation

The Panhellenic exams are a national test given each June to all Greek high school graduates who want to attend a Greek university or technical college. Competition is intense and many students fail. Families with children eligible to take the exams do everything they can to insure success, including spending large sums of money on *frontistiria* (private after-school classes) to give students the extra push needed to pass the exams. Students, when they declare their intention to take the exams, must state an *omada* or intended major. The exam covers several areas related to that major. Thus, for example a student who declares an interest in law will be examined in history, Latin, Classical Greek, a foreign language (French or English), and composition. The history exam, as well as the language exams, require vast amounts of memorization. Whole books, hundreds of pages long, have to be memorized for the history exam almost word for word.

I observed four young people (two men and two women) studying for these exams and in all cases was impressed by the degree to which preparation involved not just these individuals, but the whole family system. One adult, usually the mother, took on the role of monitor. She would set aside several hours a week to listen to her daughter or son recite texts, and to follow along with the original and correct the student as needed. The rest of the family would cooperate by giving the student as much time and space as they could. Deviations from the routine, such as a relative coming to stay, were avoided if at all possible. Unfortunately, not one of the four students I observed passed, despite the elaborate preparations and the fact that three of them were on their second try, having already failed once the year before.

Although the exams themselves exist at an institutional level, preparation for them is very much a family and informal matter. The formal system is translated into an informal one in face-to-face encounters when mothers sit down with children and rehearse pieces of history, the mothers serving as monitors and evaluators by virtue of the fact that they hold the text on which the young person models his or her recital. The mothers also offer advice about studying—mnemonic devices, priorities, and so on. The emphasis on memorization of poems, songs and TV advertisements in the early years serves young people well at this later stage, when so much of their future depends on their memory of texts.

Political Discourse

In 1986, when the data for this study were collected, the Social Democratic government (PASOK) of Andreas Papandreou was the ruling party.[9] The political climate supported a wider range of voices than had been allowed under earlier, more repressive governments, and Greeks everywhere were accustomed to vocalizing their opinions about the political situation. An abundance of newspapers ranging from far left to far right, and local to national, were available at every newsstand, even in small towns and villages. Trikala, which is not a large city, had three newspapers of its own. Conversations almost always included mention of a political topic, and women and children as well as men were interested and involved in the political process. Children were encouraged to have political opinions of their own and to practice the discourse that their elders so frequently modeled.

In October 1986, local elections for mayor were held in every major Greek town and city. In Trikala there were four candidates: Trigonis, the incumbent *PASOK* (social democrat) candidate; Papasterios, an "independent" candidate whom many claimed was really with the right wing New Democracy party; Sakkas, the *KKE Exoteriko* (External Communist Party) candidate; and Papageorgios, a *KKE Esoteriko* (Internal Communist) candidate. Four-year-old Alexis knew the names of all four and some of the parties. In a remarkable dialogue during the time the heating system was being installed in the Yorgakis home, four plumbers on their coffee break engaged Alexis in political discourse about the upcoming elections. Following is an exerpt from this discourse, in which Katerina participates as well:

---

[9]At the time this book was submitted for publication, the ruling party of Geeece had changed once again to the "New Democracy" (Nea Dhimokratia) of Karamanlis. Because this is a conservative, right-wing party, the political climate has undoubtedly changed and some of the descriptions I have provided about political life in Greece may no longer be accurate.

P1. So that's how it is, Trigonis messed it up for us, is that right?
   (*Ki'ets o Trigonis ah mas ta'kane mouskema etsi;*)
P2. Come on man
   (*Ela re*)
A. What do you think he did?
   (*Em ti ta'kane;*)
P1. Who did it right? Who said it right?
   (*Pios ta'kane kala; Pios ta'pe kala;*)
A. Sakkas
   (*O Sakkas*)
P1. Did Sakkas say it better?
   (*O Sakkas ta'pe kalitera;*)
P2. (laughs)
P1. Yes but we're going to vote for Papasterios though
   (*Nai alla emeis tha psifizoume Papasterios omos*)
A. Ohh Papasterios messed it up too I tell you
   (*Ohh kai o Papasterios ta'kane mouskema leo*)
P1. He too?
   (*Kai aftos;*)
A. Papasterios messed it up
   (*O Papasterios ta'kane mouskema*)
P1. Aah?
A. Where can I vote now?
   (*Pou boro na psifiso tora?*)
P2. O Sakkas
P1. Sakkas messed it up
   (*O Sakkas ta'kane mouskema*)
P3. No, Sakkas
   (*Ohi, o Sakkas*)
A. No
   (*Ohi*)
P1. Ah no, Sak I learned that Sakkas
   (*Ah ohi o Sak o Sakkas ego ematha*)
A. I eh I learned that Sa I learned Papasterios did
   (*Ego e ego emasa oti o Sa ego emasa o Papasterios ta'kane*)
K. Hmm how did Papasterios
   (*Hmm o Papasterios pos*)
A. Mitsotakis too[10]
   (*Kai o Mitsotakis*)
P1. Did Mitsotakis mess it up too?
   (*Ki'o Mitsotakis ta'kane thalassa;*)

---

[10]Mitsotakis was a right-wing candidate in the national elections.

K. Hey you can't corner him now you know, he makes it out that everyone's messing up, he's not with anyone, he quarrels with all (*Am dhen boreis na ton vreis tora to xer's mas thalasson aftos thedhen einai me kanenan, m'olous t'sakatei*)

A. Ooo Mitsotakis messed up too (*Ooo o Mitsotakis mouskema ki'aftos*)

P1. Now you didn't tell me, are you with Mitsotakis, Papandreou, or Florakis? (*Tora esi dhen m'eipes me to Mitsotaki eisai me to Papandreou i me ton Floraki;*)[11]

A. Aaa, with PASOK, my boy, didn't I tell you? (*Aaa, me to PASOK paidhaki mou, dhen sou'pa;*)

(Everyone laughs)

Although the teaching is less overt in this instance than in others, Alexis nonetheless seems to be learning not only about the system of knowledge surrounding political candidates and their parties, but also about how to carry on this kind of talk. He is learning the conventions of political discourse, but the adults indicate through their laughter and gentle teasing questions that this is *psemata*. The system of knowledge is considerably simplified in that political candidates in this system can only do three things: They can make a mess of things, they can do things right, and they can say things right. Most of them seem to do the first.

CONCLUSION

This chapter has portrayed four examples of declarative teaching and learning in *alitheia* frame (babyclothes, expressing emotion, radiation, and exam preparation) and two examples in *psemata* frame (kinship and political discourse). The *psemata* frame functions rather differently in these declarative examples than in the procedural ones in the previous chapter. In procedural teaching and learning, *psemata* framing creates opportunities for learners to play at performing a task without the consequences of *alitheia*; that is, without critical evaluation or fear of failure. It does this by simplifying a process, which may involve omission of components, reordering of components, or merely a rough sketch of the *alitheia* version. In declarative teaching and learning, on the other hand, *psemata* framing produces transformation of the knowledge system that is being taught. This transformation also involves simplification, but this time it is simplification of the knowledge system rather than of a process. A crucial aspect of the

---

[11]All were candidates in the national elections the following year.

knowledge system may be omitted or avoided (e.g., the differences between kinship based on blood, marriage, and symbolic connection).

The *psemata* examples in this chapter, furthermore, do not show the kind of overt verbal marking we saw in the cupping episode or the fillo rolling episode. Instead, these examples contain more subtle cues: the adults' frequent laughter in the discussion about politics, and the continual teasing style of questioning on the part of adults in both the political and the kinship episodes. In the political discussion, one of the functions of the *psemata* frame seems to be to expose the learner's state of knowledge for the sake of amusing the adults. In this case, as in many others, teaching and learning are not the primary purposes of the interaction. Rather, the interaction is constituted by other goals and only incidentally involves teaching and learning.

7 Teaching and Learning to Use Language

This chapter looks in depth at two more examples of the *psemata/alitheia* distinction in informal instruction, this time focused on language use. Language may sometimes be taught procedurally, declaratively, or as this chapter shows, by focusing on discrete points in a way that is neither procedural nor declarative.

SPEAKING RIGHT

People in Kiriakitsa and Trikala pay attention to speech and care very much how those under their sphere of influence talk. Adults often tell children to "Speak right!" (*Mila kala!*), and comment that other people's children "don't speak well" (*dhen milane kala*). There are right ways and wrong ways, beautiful ways and ugly ways, and everyone has a notion of what these are, although they may disagree. A recent description of the Modern Greek language defines the patterns of Athenian speakers as "standard" (Mackridge, 1985). Likewise, informants in my study, when asked what kind of speech was "correct," would invariably refer to Athenian speech, saying that the Athenians "complete the words" (*oloklironoune tis lexes*) and have more aesthetically pleasing pronunciation. The value informants place on the Athenian dialect is a function of prestige. Thessalian village dialects, although fully grammatical communicative systems, are seen as low prestige varieties.

Teaching children to "speak right" covers a great deal of linguistic territory from correcting mispronounced words to teaching socially appropriate styles. When children do not "speak right," other adults tend to blame the parents and grandparents for not encouraging the children to speak, or for not speaking well themselves and therefore providing poor models. Monitoring is thus extended to adults as well as children; it is not unusual to hear an 18-year-old comment on her grandmother's speech, ridiculing it affectionately as "village dialect."

One of the markers of the vernacular, often said to be disrespectful and slangy, is the term *em ti*. This expression is used when answering yes/no questions, as for example:

Question: Is your car green?
                 (*Einai prasino to aftokinito sou;*)
Response: *Em ti,* is it red?
                 (*Em ti, kokkino einai;*)

The effect is somewhat sarcastic; the respondant indicates through *em ti* that the question has an obvious affirmative answer and did not need to be asked in the first place. A response with similar effect in English might be a brusque, "What do you think, it's red?"

Em ti can also be used to agree with another person's statement:

Statement: They're looking out for their own interests
                   (*Kittan ta simferonta tous.*)
Response: What do you think they're doing?
                 (*Em ti kanoun;*)

Here the effect is less sarcastic, but still the use of *em ti* indicates a certain obviousness on the part of the first speaker.

Alexis hears *em ti* a great deal from the people closest to him. His father, mother, grandmother, and grandfather all use it. Yet it is considered impolite and sassy by some of Alexis' cousins, who have had more schooling than their parents or grandparents. The vignette that follows describes an interaction in which Alexis is corrected for using *em ti* by his 22-year-old cousin, Tonis.

Em ti

Alexis is staying with his grandparents when his cousin Tonis, a university student in Thessaloniki, comes to visit for a few hours. Tonis, the grandparents (Grigoris and Katerina), and I are sitting in the kitchen/bedroom chatting over coffee while Alexis plays with one of his toy tractors near Grigoris.

Grigoris tells Alexis to make a road (make believe) and on seeing the result says,

G. That's not a good road cars don't pass on it tractors pass, right?
   (*Aftos dhen einai kalos dhromos dhen pernan ta aftokinita pernan ta trakteria (   ) etsi;*)
A. What do you think, don't they pass?
   (*Em ti kanoun dhen pernan;*)
T. There it is again Alexi what did you just say?
   (*Na to pali Alexi ti eipes tora;*)

Tonis refers to Alexis' use of *em ti*, which he had corrected a short time earlier. Alexis replies that he had said "Don't the tractors pass?" (*Dhen pernan ta trakteria;*). Tonis tells Alexis he is being *ponyiros* (clever), in that he won't admit he used *em ti*. Katerina then joins the conversation, saying to Tonis, "Hey Antoni, you can't overcome that thing" (*Vre Antoni, dhen boreis na antimetopeis afto to pragma*). In other words, Katerina believes it is futile to try and correct this. Tonis persists, however, asking Alexis to recall what he was told about *em ti*. To this Alexis cautiously replies,

A. The *em ti* is not good.
   (*To em ti dhen einai kalo*)
T. It's not that it isn't good; it isn't nice
   (*Dhen einai dhen einai kalo; dhen einai oraio.*)

Tonis then tells Alexis not to look at him *ponyira* (cleverly). The look he refers to is a kind of sidelong glance. Katerina, however, implies that this look might be the result of too much hair in the eyes, for she says, "If his hair is cut from the bottom necessarily your mother will fix it after" (*Kourepsei ta mallia tou ap'kato anagastika i mana sou tha ta ftiaxei istera*).

Alexis insists again that he didn't say *em ti,* and Tonis tells him not to tell lies. At this point, Grigoris intervenes with a question:

G. Won't you tell me, Alexander, Alexander, shall we go to the river?
   (*Dhen mou les Alexandre, Alexandre tha pame sto potami;*)
A. Em ti—
G. Aaaap!
K. Ha haaa

Now Alexis knows he is caught. He listens to his older cousin's correction, and then in a much-lowered voice repeats, "I'll go, I'll say" (*Tha paw, tha po*). Tonis rewards him with a *Bravo* and the conversation moves on to another topic, getting bread. However, the *em ti* issue comes up twice later on, once when Alexis again "slips" and is corrected by Tonis, and second when Alexis replies to his sister, Rena, who has asked him if he wants to go back to his home in Trikala with Tonis:

A. I'll go, what will I do—will I sit/stay?
   (*Tha paw, ti tha kano—tha kathiso;*)
R. Enough clevernesses, OK
   (*As tis exipnades, etsi.*)
A. Why, did I say em ti now? Did I say it? I didn't say it.
   (*Yiati tora eipa em ti; Eipa? Dhen eipa.*)
R. You didn't say em ti but you say clevernesses
   (*Dhen eipes em ti alla les exipnades.*)

The conversation then moves to another topic, and soon after Tonis leaves. In the ensuing weeks and months, Alexis continues to hear the adults around him use *em ti* and of course to use it himself.[1]

Interpretation

Initiation.   Tonis initiates the teaching by calling attention to Alexis' speech. Each teaching episode in this conversation is in fact dependent on Alexis first saying *em ti* or something that is considered "cleverness." This perceived error and the initiation of teaching might be thought of as an "adjacency pair" (Levinson, 1983, p. 303) in that the error is always followed by the correction as long as Tonis continues to interact with Alexis in this conversation. In this sense, it is a temporary adjacency pair, a rule of speaking that operates only as long as certain people are co-present. A broader way of looking at the initiation is to see Alexis as the provider of the context. Informal instruction, as we have seen in the examples discussed earlier, rarely occurs without a prior context to which the teaching is addressed. In this episode, and other episodes that involve the teaching of language use, the teacher monitors the learner's speech, waiting for the context to appear rather than creating a lesson in and of itself.

Task Structure.   In simplest terms, the goal of the teacher, Tonis, is for Alexis to recognize the situational inappropriateness of *em ti.* This goal is related to a larger motive that has to do with Alexis' emerging social identity. The use of *em ti,* especially toward those who are not one's equals, is associated with people from villages, people who have few if any years of schooling, and people who are *manges* (see description in chapter 4). Tonis is trying to educate Alexis away from sounding like (and therefore in a sense, being) one of these kinds of people. It is noteworthy that Katerina, during this same interaction, uses *em ti* once and no one corrects her or even seems to notice. Her status is greater than or equal to all present, so when

---

[1]The full transcript of this episode appears in Appendix E.

she uses *em ti* it does not smack of insubordination or sassiness. Further-more, because of her age she is not considered "teachable" to the same extent as Alexis.

In theory, one could work toward the goal of "getting Alexis to recognize situational approriateness" through a number of different task structures. Another teacher might structure the task differently from Tonis, but still be working toward the same goal. Another way of thinking about task structure is to think about what is expected of the learner. These expecta-tions are revealed in the teacher's communication to the learner.

Tonis expects three main things of Alexis in connection with the goal:

1. Notice and admit the use of *em ti*.
2. Remember and express the awareness that *em ti* is "not nice."
3. Imitate the model.

Each of these expectations is expressed in Tonis' discourse, some of them several times. The following utterances are directed toward making Alexis admit to using *em ti*:

There it is again, Alexis; what did you just say?
(*Na to pali Alexi; ti eipes tora;*)
Come on now don't change (the topic?)
(*Ela tora min allazeis (   )*)
Don't change the topic, what did you say before?
(*Min allazeis kouvenda, ti eipes proigoumenos;*)
What did you just say? Ha ha—Now what did you say?
(*Ti eipes tora? Ha ha — Tora ti eipes;*)

The next two utterances are directed toward making Alexis remember and express awareness of situational appropriateness (see item 2):

I Alexi—what did I tell you?
(*Ego Alexi—ti sou eipa;*)
What did I tell you?
(*Ti sou eipa;*)

The next two utterances are directed toward making Alexis imitate the model (see item 3):

Say, "Yes, we'll go to the river."
(*Pes, "Nai, tha pame sto potami."*)
"Yes, we'll go" or "No, we won't go."
(*"Nai, tha pame" i "Ohi, dhen tha pame."*)

At one level the task, as Tonis communicates it, is procedural; that is, Alexis should say several things, all of which are a kind of "doing." But another part of the task is declarative, in that Alexis is expected to understand, not only to do. He is expected to have an awareness of appropriateness, monitor his own language use, and know when to apply the modelling Tonis provides.

Instructional Interaction. From the start, the interaction in this episode is conflictual. Teacher and learner do not share the same goal, as evidenced by Alexis' unwillingness to do what Tonis tells him. The pattern of interaction can be characterized broadly as a pattern of questioning and avoiding, in which Tonis does the questioning and Alexis does the avoiding. But Alexis is progressively pinned down more and more until finally he runs out of avoidance strategies and gives in.

The interaction can also be seen as a struggle between *alitheia* and *psemata*. Tonis insists on *alitheia* as the frame of interpretation, but Alexis tries to interact in a *psemata* frame. Tonis will not allow it, calling attention to every evidence of Alexis' attempt to change frames:

You're very clever.
(*Eisai poli ponyiros.*)
You're a diplomat now.
(*Eisai dhiplomatis tora.*)
Don't look at me cleverly.
(*Mi me kittas emena ponyira.*)
Don't look at me that way ah—cleverly.
(*Mi me kittas emena etsi ah—ponyira.*)
But of course—you're looking at me cleverly.
(*Ma pos—me kittas ponyira.*)
Look here—there it is—like that—you're looking at me cleverly—I see it.
(*Kitta edho—na to—etsi—me kittas ponyira ah—to vlepo.*)
Don't tell me lies—you said it.
(*Mi mou les psemata—to eipes.*)

All of these utterances call attention to Alexis' attempt to establish his own private *psemata* frame. They also call attention to a struggle of social identities, for Tonis has said of *em ti*: "It's not that it isn't good; it's not nice" (*Dhen einai then einai kalo; dhen einai oraio*).

Tonis' juxtaposition of "good" and "nice" in this utterance informs us that there is an important difference between the two adjectives that word-for-word translation obscures. Subsequent interviewing about this difference revealed that *kalo* in this utterance means "grammatical" or "understandable"; in other words, the utterance has a meaning and that meaning can be understood. *Oraio,* on the other hand, means that the utterance is aesthetically correct or appropriate to the social situation. Thus, Tonis is contrasting two kinds of utterances that are unacceptable: those that do not make grammatical sense and those that are situationally inappropriate.

Of course Tonis and Alexis are not the only participants in this interaction. The roles of Grigoris and Katerina must be considered too. Their roles can best be understood as supportive of one or the other side. Katerina makes her allegiance clear twice, first when she says, "Hey Toni, you can't do anything about that thing" (*Vre Toni, dhen boreis na antimetopeis afto to pragma*), and second when she refers to Alexis' long hair as though offering it as a possible reason for his "clever" looks. In both instances, she tries to see things from the child's point of view, and manages to communicate this allegiance without contradicting the basic content of Tonis' teaching. She is perhaps the most experienced diplomat of all. Grigoris on the other hand collaborates with Tonis, as shown in his "entrapment" of Alexis. He creates a question which Alexis is almost sure to answer with *em ti* and thus contributes to proving Tonis' point.

Relationship Between Learner's Zone of Proximal Development and Teaching.   Language teachers and learners are familiar with the distinction between competence (what a learner knows) and performance (what a learner does). They know that performance generally lags behind competence, that learners know more than they can spontaneously produce. However, the reasons why certain things take longer to produce are not clearly understood. Many factors can influence a learner's ability and willingness to produce what he or she knows, including age, type of input, grammatical complexity, various types of interference (in the case of second language learners) and affective and social variables. The problem with *em ti* is a problem of competence versus performance in so far as Alexis has heard that it is not nice but has not made this knowledge part of his active language production. There are several indicators that his awareness has increased. These include his ability to repeat what Tonis had told him (that the *em ti* is not nice), his somewhat defeated-sounding agreement when he says "I'll go, I'll say" (*Tha pao, tha po*), and later, his challenge to his sister Rena when she accuses him of saying "clevernesses" (Why, did I say *em ti* now? Did I say it? I didn't say it.).

Although he demonstrates his learning of the "subject matter" in these ways he continues to use *em ti* after this episode is over. There are several possible explanations for this. One is that he has not yet applied his cognitive understanding to his active use of language, and so it is just a matter of time, and perhaps helpful prodding from the adults around him, before he will monitor his own speech in such a way that he catches himself before the *em ti* comes out. However, this explanation ignores the reasons he learned *em ti* in the first place.

Most of his primary caretakers use *em ti*. This input in itself is a major reason for him to continue its use. The message that Tonis gives him conflicts with the world as he knows it. That world is much closer to him and more immediate than the world Tonis represents — the world of a new, university-educated generation of young people. Alexis sees Tonis only rarely and so can have little motivation to change his speaking habits to please a family member who is away most of the time.

Then there is also the matter of affect and social identity. Using *em ti* among others who use it promotes feelings of solidarity and at the same time a certain power through its sarcasm. These can be viewed as definite advantages.

Tonis' teaching is aimed more toward Alexis' performance than toward his competence. By monitoring, pointing out errors, questioning, and modeling, he tries to simplify Alexis' role in the learning process. He refuses to simplify the task itself, insisting that Alexis ultimately perform all the different parts. Thus, the interaction is more characteristic of scaffolding than shaping.

PRONUNCIATION LESSONS

Another frequently corrected aspect of language in this community is children's pronunciation of difficult words. Caretakers become familiar with the words that a particular child has trouble with, and then focus on these, monitoring and correcting the child's use of the words in an effort to move the child from babytalk toward a more adult kind of talk. Different caretakers correct for different aspects of language. In Alexis' case, Katerina corrected his pronunciation whereas Grigoris, Tonis, and other more educated relatives corrected the more social aspects such as *em ti* in the previous discussion.

The list of frequently mispronounced words that Katerina focused on are shown in Table 5.

In the following vignette, Katerina focuses on *trapezi, karekla,* and *trakteri*. What is most interesting about this interaction is the way she frames her teaching. Her typical pattern is to simply correct errors in Alexis' speech immediately after he has uttered them by modeling the correct pronunciation and then directing him to repeat the model, as in, "Karekla — you say it too" (*Karekla — yia pes to kai si*). In this episode however, she frames the interaction differently.

TABLE 5
Frequently Mispronounced Words

Correct	Incorrect	Translation
karekla	kaleta/kaleka	chair
trapezi	tapezi	table
trakteri	trater/trateri	tractor
porta	borta	door
paithakia	paizakia	children
dhromo	dhomo	road
xaplono	klaposo	I lie down
strava	stava	crooked
asanser	saser	elevator

Trapezi

It is October 14, 1986, and Katerina, Alexis, and I are on the back porch of the Yorgakis house in the village Kiriakitsa. Alexis is playing with some toy vehicles (tractor, helicopter, cars) and particularly with a toy tractor that he is using to "plow the field" like Grandpa. Katerina and I are sitting near him. Grigoris, Katerina's husband, is within earshot but does not participate in this particular episode. Just before the episode begins, however, Grigoris says something to me about moving a table, thus providing the first mention of what Katerina later uses as an opportunity for teaching. The body of the episode consists of Katerina and Alexis exchanging roles several times with the goal of improving Alexis' control over certain word pronunciations, the first of which is *trapezi* or table.

The game begins as follows:

K. I'm Alexi and I say "tapezi."
   (*Ego t'Alexi leo "tapezi."*)
A. no
   (*ohi*)
K. You, how do you say it?
   (*Esi pos to les;*)
A. Grandma, I don't want you to become little.
   (*Yiayioula, le selo na yineis mikri.*) [2]

Alexis and Katerina proceed to play a game in which they trade roles. When Katerina is big and Alexis is little (their *alitheia* roles) Alexis makes mistakes in pronunciation. When Katerina is little and Alexis is big

---

[2] *le selo* is a mispronunciation of *dhen thelo*.

(*psemata* frame), Katerina makes the mistakes and Alexis is supposed to correct her.

These are the assumptions of the game, but Alexis resists. He does not want his grandmother to be little. When she continues to play little and to ask him how to say *tapezi* he asks her, "Grandma, didn't you eat yet?" (*Yiayia, dhen efages akoma;*). He is referring here to the common plea of Greek caretakers (and probably most other caretakers as well) to their children, "Eat to grow big" (*Faei na megaloseis*). Katerina replies affirmatively, and produces a correct pronunciation of *trapezi*. Alexis then asks her what she said, and rather than repeating, she asks him to tell her—"You say it too" (*Yia pes to kai 'si*). He imitates her correctly, and she confirms by repeating it again.

Then Katerina introduces a new pronunciation problem, again in *psemata* frame. She pretends she is little and mispronounces *karekla* (chair) as *kaleka*. Alexis once again urges her to eat, but she insists that he tell her the correct pronunciation first. He does so, but shortly afterward states clearly "Now I have become little" (*Tora egina mikros*) and begins making tractor noises. Katerina tries one more word, *trakteri* (tractor), this time presenting it correctly in her "big" role. Alexis does not pronounce it correctly after her, and from there he succeeds in diverting her attention by asking her what the *trater* did (it plowed a field).[3]

Interpretation

Initiation.   The first overt act leading to teaching and learning in this scene comes when Katerina says to Alexis: "I'm Alexis and I say tapezi." This seems out of context if we look only at the preceding utterance, in which Alexis asks his grandfather when they will plow the field again but gets no answer. Earlier, however, Grigoris had in fact mentioned the word "table" and this must have triggered in Katerina an association with Alexis' current "difficult words."

Katerina's statement, "I'm Alexis and I say *tapezi,*" functions not only as an initiation of teaching, but also as a shifting of roles. In its function as a marker of role shift, it tells us first that Katerina will take on some aspect of Alexis' behavior. The second part of the statement tells us exactly which aspect of his behavior she is going to take on (i.e., his pronunciation of the word *trapezi* as *tapezi*). At this point it is not yet clear *why* she is initiating a role switch (i.e., it could be simply to make fun of Alexis' childish pronunciation), but in her next utterance it becomes clear that she is using this as a teaching strategy, for she asks Alexis, "How do you say it?" Thus, the initiation of teaching really takes place across two of Katerina's turns; it is implied in the first, and overtly completed in the second.

This initiation, because it co-occurs with the role switch, also establishes

---

[3]The full transcript of this episode appears in Appendix E.

TABLE 6
Role Switches and Topic Changes

Round 1		Round 2		Round 3		Round 4		Round 5
Alitheia		Psemata		Alitheia		Psemata		Alitheia
A little		A big		A little		A big		A little
K big		K little		K big		K little		K big
	K switches		K switches		K switches		A switches	
		trapezi				karekla		trakteri[4]

the *psemata* frame. (Role switching, it was noted chapter 4, is one of the ways to establish *psemata* framing.) Thus, in this episode, teaching and learning begin at the same time that *psemata* framing begins. Unlike the kinship episode discussed in the previous chapter, here all participants are aware of the *psemata* frame; there is no "fabrication," benign or otherwise.

Task Structure.   Once again, the task in this episode is constituted primarily through talk, and so it is in talk that we can find the elements of its structure.

Katerina and Alexis appear to share a similar concept of the goal of their activity. The goal is for Alexis to practice saying the words right, but at the same time to have a little fun. The structure of the task is built on two devises—the role switching game and changes in topic, which are actually changes in the focal words. The role switches and topic changes can be depicted as shown in Table 6.

The task of "saying the words right" can thus be decomposed into different roles or different topics, but it cannot be decomposed as a process for the task is not structured as a series of steps. Nor is it possible, based on this interaction, to delineate a knowledge system that is being communicated. The teaching and learning is based on discrete teaching points (i.e., words to be pronounced correctly) and the structure of the task is determined by the changes from one discrete point to the next or from one role assignment to another.

In the previous two chapters, the *psemata* frame was closely associated with type of teaching. That is, in the cupping episode, the *psemata* frame functioned to transform a process (thus lending credence to the idea that procedural teaching was involved); in the kinship episode, the *psemata* frame functioned to transform a knowledge system (albeit without the learner's awareness). Here however, neither process nor knowledge system are being transformed. Instead, the roles and social identities of the participants are changed.

---

[4] Katerina initiates all topic changes (i.e., changes in focal words)

TABLE 7
Cues Based on Association with "Big" or "Little"

Big (expert or teacher)	Little (novice or learner)
Says *trapezi*	Says *tapezi*
Says *karekla*	Says *kaleta* or *kaleka*
Says *tpakteri*	Says *tater* or *trater*
Eats food to grow big	Has not eaten yet
	Makes tractor noises (*tuka tuka . . .*)

Instructional Interaction. Because the roles of teacher and learner are not consistent in this interaction, participants have to cue each other so that they know who is playing what role at a given moment. These cues seem to be mutually agreed upon through previous interaction, and are now shared knowledge to be relied upon in the present interaction. Table 7 shows a list of the cues based on their association with "big" or "little."

The tractor noises, it should be noted, are a very frequent part of Alexis' everyday play. In fact, he has a large repertoire of vehicle noises that he can produce. He can differentiate vocally among tractors, cars, buses, helicopters, ambulances, police cars, bulldozers, and cement trucks. Besides signifying particular kinds of vehicles, these noises also signify that Alexis is in a "little" frame, or at least this transcript suggests so; he stops using the tractor noises when he "becomes big," and starts using them again when he returns to "little": "Ah, now I became little. *Tukou tukou tuk tuk tuk . . .*"

Alexis' performance is evaluated each time Katerina corrects him. Due to the role play, however, Alexis himself also becomes an evaluator. When he takes the role of the "big person," Katerina is in effect asking him to correct or evaluate her. Thus, we see another effect of the role-play situation: It leads participants to become more self-evaluating by taking charge of their own monitoring and correction process.

This episode recalls some of the devises used in Grigoris' and Thomas' verbal interaction with Alexis in the cupping and dancing episodes. Directives like "Hey, you say it" (*Yia pes to 'si*) and variations on this are similar to "Go on, put again" (*Ante vale pali*) in that they both direct the learner to do something. The difference is that the action here is verbal, whereas in the earlier examples it was physical.

Relation Between Learner's Zone of Proximal Development and Teaching. Because Katerina interacts with Alexis almost every day, she is very well attuned to his level of competence and performance; she knows almost exactly what he does and doesn't know. As a result, she is is able to key her teaching to his zone of proximal development. In this instance, she knows that Alexis already has in his competence a knowledge of the correct and incorrect pronunciations of *trapezi, karekla,* and *trakteri.* The problem she is seeking to adjust is one of performance, not competence. She uses role play as an advanced teaching strategy to encourage practice in the performance aspect of Alexis' language development.

Alexis himself is aware of and able to recognize "babytalk"; in fact, the whole game that he and Katerina play would not be possible without this recognition. However, although he clearly demonstrates competence in recognizing and correcting his own babytalk, he is not ready to give it up entirely or to take on the role of "big person" in relation to Katerina's "little person": "Grandma, I don't want you to become little." He has definite ideas about his own zone of proximal development and communicates what he is and is not ready to do. This episode does not involve the introduction of new knowledge to Alexis. He is not being pushed into the zone of proximal development. Rather, Katerina sets up a situation through the *psemata* frame whereby he can practice his performance as though it were a game, with role switching being the main transformation. This is shaping in yet another form.

COMPARISON

These two episodes both involve teaching and learning the use of the first language, although in one case the subject is social register and in the other pronunciation. The two episodes defy categorization as either procedural or declarative. They are neither taught as processes (which can be decomposed) nor as knowledge systems (which can be seen as a set of logically related parts). Yet elements of procedural teaching appear in both in that the learner is directed to say certain things, and saying is a kind of doing. There is also something declarative in both episodes; in *em ti* the learner is expected to remember a rule and monitor his own speech, and in *trapezi* he is expected to know what constitutes babytalk. However, the two episodes are most alike in that they both involve teaching and learning of a single item or discrete point.

The same learner appears in both episodes, but the teachers are different—a university-educated cousin, and a grandmother with 3 years of schooling. Still, all participants are part of the inner network that includes close family members and neighbors.

The *em ti* episode is conflictual in that teacher and learner do not share the same goals. Tonis wants Alexis to monitor his use of *em ti*, but Alexis cannot see any good reason for this except that Tonis wills it, and Tonis is not present often enough to have any great influence. The *trapezi* episode, on the other hand, does not involve any conflict, except in so far as Alexis does not want his grandmother to be "little." He plays along willingly, however.

Both episodes manifest a tension between *psemata* and *alitheia* framing. In *Em ti* it is the learner who wants to establish a covert *psemata* frame, but although he tries he is faced each time with the teacher's more powerful *alitheia* frame, and thus *alitheia* persists as the main frame of interpretation. In *Trapezi* we see a more playful tension between frames in that both teacher and learner see frame changing as part of the game they are playing. Either partner in this interaction has a right to initiate a frame change, although in fact Katerina does so first and most often. Through this modeling, she may also be teaching Alexis how to shift frames.

Finally, the *em ti* episode is characteristic of scaffolding in that the teacher holds the task constant and intervenes to help the learner in the completion of the task. *Trapezi* is more characteristic of shaping, for although the task remains unchanged, Alexis is not challenged to learn something new or difficult but rather to practice and improve what he already knows.

OTHER DISCRETE-POINT TEACHING AND LEARNING

Kale/Re

Kale and *re* are two ways of addressing people in Greek conversation.[5] The closest translations in English are "dear"[6] for *kale,* and "man" *for re.* They may be followed directly by a proposition, or they may be followed by a name or other form of address and then a proposition, as in "Dear Vasili, why don't you wait and we'll go tomorrow?" (*Kale Vasili, yiati dhen perimeneis na pame avrio;*). *Re,* like *em ti,* is considered disrespectful and slangy as well as *mangika* (the language of the *manges,* discussed in chapter 4). Also like *em ti,* however, it appears with high frequency in much village conversation and functions as a token of intimacy among people who are not trying to maintain social distance. Thus a child reads two conflicting messages in the social environment: (a) that people around him use *re* frequently, and (b) that some people tell him it is not nice to use *re.*

When a speaker uses *re* inappropriately (i.e., when the listener is demanding more social distance and respect) a formulaic response is available:

"Say *re* to your mother and father, not to me."
(*Re na peis tin mana sou kai ton patera sou, ohi emena.*)

---

[5]There is a third variant, *vre,* which for the purposes of this brief discussion is being subsumed under *re.* It is, however, slightly less slangy than *re.*

[6]The literal translation of *kale* is "good one," but because we do not use this in English I have substituted the more standard term *dear.*

On the other hand, a speaker can create a sense of solidarity by using *re,* but as one interviewee pointed out, "The other person has to accept the *re*" (*Prepei na to dhehthei o allos to re*).

Alexis uses *re* liberally with both intimates and nonintimates. At times no one comments on this, and at other times it becomes a focal point for correction and teaching. The most frequent teacher on this point was Grigoris, Alexis' grandfather. I recorded numerous examples of his corrections on audio and videotape, in the midst of conversations and activities focused on other things. The corrections of *re,* like those of *em ti,* appeared only in the context of an "error"; that is, Alexis had to say *re* in order for the teaching to occur. The episodes were usually very brief, comprising only a few utterances at the most. For example, in the following exchange Alexis is at his grandparents' house talking on the telephone with his father while Grigoris and Katerina listen:

A. *Re* Daddy (*Re Baba*)
G. Kale Daddy (*Kale Baba*)
A. Eeh, I don't know that (*Eeh, dhen to xero afto*)
K. He doesn't know that? (*Dhen to xer'afto;*)
G. Ah, what do you know, *re* halvah ah? (*Ah ti xer's re halva ah;*)
A. *Kale* Daddy (*Kale Baba*)
G. *Kale* Daddy (*Kale Baba*)
A. Eeh, I didn't know it (*Eeh, dhen to'xera*)
G. *Kale* Daddy (*Kale Baba*)
A. Yes (*Nai*)

During these correction sequences, the adult who is doing the correcting always insists on the *alitheia* frame, even though Alexis may try to pretend that he "doesn't know that." The adult presses him until he produces the desired utterance with *kale* instead of *re.* Note, however, that Grigoris himself uses *re* when he calls Alexis a "halvah."

Here, as with the other discrete-point examples, the teacher is neither decomposing a process nor delineating a system of knowledge. The object of teaching and learning is a single item, and although it belongs to a much more complicated system of social register, the teacher does not overtly point to it as part of that larger system. He refers only to the single item, not to the system of which it is a part. Thus, no breakdown of knowledge or process occurs, only a repetitive drilling of one item.

In the previous interaction, we see evidence of Alexis' development of monitored speech in his shift from "Eeh, I don't know that" to a few turns later, "Eeh, I didn't know that." In other words, he knows it now, for the moment at least. This development of monitoring, however, does not result in his no longer saying *re.* Rather, it is a continuing process stretching over many months, perhaps years. In this process, he learns that *re* is a marked item that carries important social meanings.

Sou Eipa/Soupa

In constrast to the *alitheia* frame in which *re* is corrected and replaced with *kale,* the standard form of "I told you" (*sou eipa*) was taught in *psemata* frame on at least one occasion.

Speakers of the village dialect often contract *sou eipa* to *soupa,* which sounds exactly like the Greek word for soup. Alexis uses the latter form almost exclusively. One afternoon I observed his older sister Rena correcting this by purposely pretending to misunderstand him. When Alexis said *soupa,* meaning "I told you," Rena asked him, "Do you want to eat soup?" (*Theleis na fas soupa;*). As long as Alexis repeated his statement using *soupa,* Rena continued to "misunderstand," until finally she offered him a way out: "Maybe you mean to say *sou eipa*?" (*Mipos theleis na peis sou eipa;*). Alexis then repeated his statement in standard form.

It is difficult to say to what extent Alexis believed his sister's misunderstanding was real. Was he, in other words, contained by the *psemata* frame, or was he a party to it? This observation is based on fieldnotes only, so it is not possible to go back and check for evidence of his awareness on audio or videotape. In either case, however, *psemata* frame is at least used by the teacher to create the impression that a real misunderstanding might occur as a result of Alexis' use of the dialect form. Rather than appealing to appropriateness or aesthetics (as Tonis did when he said "I didn't say that *em ti* is not good; I said it's not *nice*"), Rena appeals to a referential problem to motivate Alexis to correct his usage, implying that the child's meaning will not be understood.

CONCLUSION

The fact that all of these episodes revolve around language should not be taken as a statement that discrete-point teaching does not occur in other domains, but rather that this type of teaching did not occur frequently or saliently in other domains. Furthermore, I am not implying that language use is only taught by discrete point in this community. On the contrary, I observed many occasions when language use (in the broad sense of discourse genres, literacy skills, etc.) was taught procedurally or declaratively as a whole, integrated system. For example, the television ad for "Soufflan" laundry detergent is a type of discourse taught as a procedure (First you say A, then B, then C . . .); the political discourse is taught as a knowledge system (certain candidates make a mess of things, others say it right, and others do it right). Discrete-point teaching highlights a particular piece of a bigger system and focuses the teaching on that one piece. We cannot predict what form the instruction would take were the participants to include more of the system; it could become either procedural or declarative.

The functions of *psemata* framing in these examples are qualitatively different from its functions in procedural and declarative instruction. Because the teaching does not deal directly with a process or a knowledge system, there is little to be simplified, omitted, or reordered. If anything, complexity is added. In the *trapezi* episode, Katerina introduces role switching as a kind of game to motivate Alexis. This is certainly more complicated than staying in their everyday roles, for now Alexis has to attend not only to the fact that his speech is being corrected, but also to the fact that his grandmother is pretending to be him and he is supposed to pretend to be her. The cognitive demands are increased rather than decreased. Likewise, in the *sou eipa* example, Rena complicates matters by not merely correcting Alexis, but also engaging him in a game that requires him to recognize the relationship between his mispronunciation and the word "soup." Again, more cognitive stretching rather than less is demanded.

Another point, illustrated in the *trapezi* episode, is that *psemata* framing can occur within as well as across teaching and learning episodes. All of the examples examined up to this point have covered whole episodes. Here we see how the *psemata* frame can be negotiated by the participants within an episode, moving from *alitheia* to *psemata* and back again to *alitheia* as often as the participants agree to switch roles.

In both the *trapezi* and the *sou eipa* examples, we see adults testing the smartness of children in a culturally patterned way. Readers may recall what one of the women I interviewed said when asked how one can recognize a smart child:

"You go to trick [or tease] the child, and s/he says 'No.'"
(*Esi pas na ton xeyelaseis to paidhi, kai sou leei "ohi."*)

This is exactly what Katerina and Rena do in these interactions with Alexis. They test Alexi's zone of proximal development by finding out whether he is savvy to their teasing. If so, he is not only "smart" but also beyond the level of development where the adult can still tease him about that particular thing. These teasings in which the child "gets it" can be contrasted with teasings in which the child eventually has to be told he is being teased, such as the nettle incident and the incident when Katerina points out to Alexis that his father is kidding him about sleeping outdoors (both in chapter 4).

Chapters 4, 5, 6, and 7 have shown that the *psemata* frame can be both object and mediator of learning in this community. It is an object in the sense that children growing up in this community need to know how to manipulate the *alitheia/psemata* distinction successfully, and therefore it needs to be taught through a variety of covert as well as overt methods. It is a mediator in that it frames social interaction through which knowledge is transformed from the interpersonal to the intrapersonal plane. Children learn to distinguish *alitheia* from *psemata* through the process of their own learning experiences, as well as through observing the distinction in use outside the self.

8 The Particular and the General

With whichever teacher you sit, such are the letters you will learn. (*Me opion daskalo tha katseis, tetoia grammata tha matheis.*)

—Greek proverb

This book began with a child learning to ring a doorbell, affording us entry into a particular and local world of everyday teaching and learning activities. But to stay inside this world would be to forego wider perspectives. This last chapter explores what some of these perspectives might be.

The participants in informal teaching and learning hold the key to our understanding of it, for if, as Vygotsky and other Soviet theorists insist, all cognitive development is social in origin, different players will influence the cognitive structures that are acquired. Or as the Greek proverb tells us, "With whichever teacher you sit, such are the letters you will learn." In this study, the neighborhood and the social relations among neighbors constrained to a large extent the access children and adults had to learning situations. The majority of the episodes I observed involved Alexis as learner and immediate family members as teachers, including his grandfather, grandmother, father, and cousin. The episode with Eleni and Soula demonstrated informal teaching and learning between members of different neighborhood households. Because Eleni's baby was a major attraction among the neighborhood children, parents such as Soula were frequently pulled to Eleni's house to collect their children. This created a natural opportunity for dialogue between the experienced and inexperienced mother.

Without these comfortable interchanges whose purposes are built into the fabric of everyday life, informal teaching and learning is very unlikely to occur. Because of the restricted social relations among Karagounides, Vlachs, and Gypsies, I observed no informal instruction among these groups. Likewise, unless there was a direct family connection, opportunities

150

for informal teaching and learning between villagers and townspeople were rare.

Because the participants in informal teaching and learning knew each other well, they were able for the most part to work within the learners' "zone of proximal development." Some did so better than others, however. Katerina was a better judge of Alexis' readiness to learn than, for example, Thomas in the cupping episode. This finely tuned understanding of where learners are is often missing in school, particularly when teachers do not share the culture or the language of the children. How can teachers know what students are capable of grasping if the knowledge students display is not seen as knowledge? (Jerry Lipka, personal communication, April 25, 1991). Informal teaching and learning, because it so often emerges in close personal relationships, is far more likely to take place within the zone of proximal development than formal teaching and learning.

Although the study focused on informal teaching and learning outside of school, formal kinds of order appeared in several of the episodes. Likewise, elements of informal order appear in schools whenever teachers and students meet face to face in situations that are not structured by the curriculum. Thus, the supposed dichotomy of informal and formal education is really only a convenient way of drawing a line between education that tends toward the formal, and education that tends toward the informal. In actuality, the two kinds of order are often intertwined.

Some of the most valuable learning students receive at school comes through informal channels. In graduate school, for example, this learning includes tips about how to manage the social structures of education, how to publish, how to get a job, whom to meet, which conferences to go to. Some of this comes from professors, some from peers. Unfortunately, because the channels through which informal teaching and learning take place are particularly susceptible to cultural differences, there are inequities in the availability of knowledge. The more "advantaged" students (i.e., those whose home culture is valued in the school) are presented with opportunities for informal learning, whereas those whose home culture is different tend to be shut out from these opportunities. Schools in many areas are making efforts to see that the overt curriculum is accessible to all students, but the "hidden curriculum" that is transmitted through informal processes has yet to be addressed.

The study can also help us refine the notion of conflict in education. Studies that have documented conflict in culturally incongruous situations reveal for the most part conflict over a communicative code or cueing system; people are miscommunicating with each other, misreading signs. An African-American child in a classroom with a mainstream White teacher may not see the significance of a question to which the questioner knows the answer; people in the child's home community do not ask those kinds of questions. A Hawaiian child may learn to read better when the teacher incorporates the Hawaiian "talk story" participation structure in the classroom. Some educators therefore try to align the educational process more closely with what the children are used to so that learning of content is not hampered by interference from signaling systems gone awry. These educational interventions often work very well, the Kamehameha Early Education Project being an excellent example.

Yet we should be cautious about assuming that cultural incongruity always brings conflict. Some schools, noted in chapter 1, are very effective although the style of teaching is purposely not congruous with the children's home interaction. Similarly, although it may be tempting to assume that conflict will not occur in culturally congruous situations, the episodes examined here tell us otherwise. Conflict can occur over content, as we saw in the babyclothes episode when a modern practice was perceived as a threat to a traditional one. It can occur over a difference in goals, as for example when Tonis and Alexis disagreed about the goal of saying/not saying *em ti*. Finally, conflicts over framing can occur when one person views the interaction as *psemata*, whereas the other construes it as *alitheia*. This was the case in the beginning of the cupping episode when Thomas pretended that he was going to perform "the real thing" on Alexis, who became very frightened because he believed his father.

The finding that conflict of these kinds occurs in culturally congruous situations has implications for both theory and educational practice. It suggests that we need to specify the *kinds* of conflict that occur in educational encounters, rather than referring to conflict in generic terms. Certain combinations of people and activities are associated with certain kinds of conflict; culturally different pairs of teachers and learners seem especially predisposed toward conflict over participation structure and communicative process, whereas culturally similar pairs tend to experience conflict over content, goal, or frame.

The study also raises questions about the theory of activity and its ability to explain the cognitive tasks involved in different types of informal teaching and learning. Although chapter 5 showed that the different levels of activity articulated by Leont'ev (1979) (activity, action, and operations) map quite well onto procedural tasks, the relevance of these levels to declarative and discrete-point tasks is less obvious. The declarative tasks described in the babyclothes and kinship episodes appear to be more complex than the model allows for in that they involve embeddings of reasons, consequences, and other types of logical connections. These are very different from the subtasks or operations that learners need to acquire in order to carry out dancing or cupping. The discrete-point episodes (*Em ti* and *Trapezi*) also map poorly onto the levels of activity, although for a different reason. In this case, the discreteness of the task sets it apart from a larger context or activity; the action and its operations can be described, but at the next higher level, the activity and its accompanying motivation are either missing or inexplicit. These problems do not challenge the overall integrity of the theory of activity, but they do suggest that further refinement of the levels of activity would be useful if the theory is to be relevant for a full range of educational tasks.

What have the learners learned in these episodes? In answering this question, we come face to face with the complexity of displaying informal teaching and learning in their cultural setting. Like schooling, informal teaching and learning have a "hidden curriculum." In both situations, although the most overt teaching may focus on content or subject matter, the processes of teaching also communicate important information to the learner. In the cupping scene, for example, Alexis was learning many things, cupping being only the most visible. Less visible but no less important were other lessons: First, he was learning the discourse that typically surrounds and supports cupping. For instance, one verbally marks the transition from cupping to rubdown; one engages in brief questions and answers as to whether the process hurts; one can express frustration over a torch that won't stay lit; and one closes the session by saying "O.K., you're all done now" or something to that effect and receives a "Thank you" in return. Second, Alexis was also learning about how husbands behave toward their wives, a very interesting issue to him personally as his dialogue with his mother showed. Third, he was learning about *psemata* and *alitheia* framing and the fact that in his community *psemata* has connotations of play, fun, and unserious, as well as the core connotation of lying. The *psemata* frame provided an acceptable, culturally congruent means for him to take on the untrue role of the husband/healer.

Learning about *psemata* and *alitheia* framing involves learning to recognize frames and switch frames, and this requires that certain conventions be learned, such as naming the frame, role switching, laughter, teasing questions, and the use of babytools. These conventions, however, may be dropped in adult life, for the *aghona* or struggle is not carried out in the language of *psemata* conventions. Rather, it involves unmediated confrontation with people whom one cannot trust, people who do not give warning of a change in frame.

The conventions provide scaffolding that prepares the learner to cope with the *aghona* of later life. Because the conventions of *psemata* can be elaborated to be overt (e.g., naming the frame), or reduced to function subtly (e.g., teasing questions), they allow for a range of scaffolding depending on the level of the learner and his or her immediate responses in interaction. In other words, the teacher can construct the scaffold in response to the situation. The implicit goal is that the scaffold will one day be unnecessary, and the learner will then be equipped to carry out the *aghona.* Until that time, adults and experts constantly test and probe to see how clever (*ponyiros*) the learner has become and to what extent he or she can call the bluffs of others. Thus, there were times when children were not provided with any of the conventions beforehand, as for example when Thomas told Alexis he would have to sleep outside. Alexis was not certain whether to take this seriously or not. His grandmother, seeing his uncertainty, provided the scaffolding after the fact: "Your father is putting you on. Tell him, 'Why should I go outside?'" In the world of grown-ups, one isn't normally given such advice; one simply gets duped, exploited, or ridiculed.

Learning to cope with the *aghona,* then, is a multi-tiered process. Like many language functions such as requesting and directing, its roots can be found very early in children's interactions with adults, even before talk emerges as a primary means of communication. Friedl's example of a mother pulling her breast away from the child is an earlier form of the *psemata* interactions seen in this study. These interactions are themselves constructed at different levels of difficulty. It is the graduated participation in these different degrees and kinds of *psemata* framing, from overt to almost invisible, that prepares novices in this community for their roles as agonists.

Foreigners who intend to stay in the community must also be taught, although having learned other habits in their own countries makes them less tractable than local children; I was frequently told not to trust others too easily, to be on my guard. In fact, Greeks use a derivative of the word American, *Amerikanaki,* to describe people who are naïve, gullible, or overly trusting. This word is applied to fellow Greeks as well as to North Americans.

Psemata framing has different functions in this community depending on what level of learning we look at. At the level of the most visible learning (e.g., the cupping itself), *psemata* framing shapes the experience of the learner, limiting or reducing the cognitive or physical complexity of the task so that the learner can experience success. At the level of the less visible learning, the interplay of *psemata* and *alitheia* provides a subtly graduated curriculum that teaches learners how to function in the *aghona.*

Thus, learning through *psemata* and *alitheia* frames both reflects and reinforces the general theme of *aghona.* A strong articulation exists between particular scenes and larger life. And although initially learners have to live with a certain amount of unpredictability and inconsistency (e.g. they cannot really trust their elders, as Friedl pointed out), later on this transitional state of *aghona* is resolved when learners find that the low level testing and teasing have helped prepare them for the deeper struggles of Greek adulthood.

But *psemata* framing is not the exclusive property of Greece nor of the community where I lived. Everywhere in the world, people tease each other, juxtapose play and the real thing, and in various other ways manipulate the interpretation of reality. In Trikala and Kiriakitsa, the interplay has particular cultural configurations; in other places, the distinction between play and the real thing will fit differently in the larger culture.

Psemata framing, as the analyses show, has cognitive consequences. It is a culturally coherent way of adapting tasks so that novices can participate. With this in mind, it would be valuable to study whether and how the *psemata* frame may be used in schools. When are activities framed as serious and when are they framed as play or not serious? Who does the framing and how? Do students have any rights to change the dominant frame of interpretation? If there is *psemata* framing in schools, what functions does it serve? And how is it different from what I saw in Kiriakitsa and Trikala?

Instruction, it is clear from the study, can be framed differently depending on the community, the participants, and the situation, and while the specifics of *psemata* framing explored here may be unique, the impact of local interpretive frames on cognitive activity is not. Frames are part of the social situation within which cognition takes place. To talk about situated cognition, we must also talk about the ways in which frames simultaneously shape instructional tasks and teach learners about culturally coherent ways of using frames.

Appendix A:
Variation in Informal Teaching and Learning
($n = 109$)

Age:	Adult/Child[a]		Adult/Adult		Child/Child		
	68		25		16		= 109
	(62%)		(23%)		(15%)		= 100%

Schooling:	6 Yrs. or fewer[b]		More than 6 Yrs.		Mixed		
	45		10		54		= 109
	(41%)		(9%)		(50%)		= 100%

Lifestyle:	R/R c[c]	U/U	R/U		R/C		
	14	36	29		30		= 109
	(13%)	(33%)	(26.6%)		(27.5%)		= 100%

Network:	Within Network			Between Networks			
	96			13			= 109
	(88%)			(12%)			= 100%

Formality:	Least Formal			Somewhat Formal			
	93			16			= 109
	(85%)			(15%)			= 100%

Frame:	Alitheia			Psemata			
	77			32			= 109
	(71%)			(29%)			= 100%

Type of Teaching:	Procedural		Declarative		Mixed		
	42		35		32		= 109
	(39%)		(32%)		(29%)		= 100%

Typicality:	Prototypical			Typical			
	52			57			= 109
	(48%)			(52%)			= 100%

[a]Anyone 14 or under is considered a child in this table. Also, the slash between adult and child merely means that there is at least one adult and one child in the main teaching and learning roles; there may be more than one.

[b]"Six years or less" refers to all major participants in the interaction, as does "More than 6 years." Six years was chosen as a cut-off point because that is the number of years of elementary school in Greece.

[c]R = Rural; U = Urban; C = Commuter (i.e., lives in village but works in town, or lives part time in both)

Appendix B:
Features of Prototypical Informal Teaching and Learning

1. An initiation that establishes shared focus

This could be: a. An attentional vocative (e.g., "Come mother, we're starting.")

b. Expert calling attention to novice error (e.g., "*Karekla,* good one . . .")

c. Novice question (e.g., "Why do you call her 'Mama'?")

d. Expert calling attention to problem (e.g., "The baby's going to get too hot in those clothes.")

e. Expert challenging novice (e.g., "You can't reach it.")

f. Expert or novice establishing *psemata* (not serious) frame of interpretation

g. Gestural initiation (e.g., hand gesture to indicate 'come here.')

2. Maintenance of shared central focus

Evidence in: a. Gaze orientation and postural position (observation is made possible this way)

b. Topic (both/all persons talking about same topic — use of repetition and deictic and anaphoric expressions can provide linguistic evidence of shared topic)

3. Expert's (E's) Intent to teach (teach = facilitate increase in knowledge or expertise in novice (N))

Evidence in: **Utterance Level:**

a. E telling (e.g., "We do this, then we do that")

b. E directing (e.g., "Do like this")

c. E correcting (e.g., "Not like that, like this")

d. E modeling (linguistic model, e.g., "Ka-re-kla")

Nonverbal Communication:

a. E modeling (physical or visual model)

b. E simplifying task for N (e.g., providing baby-sized or play representation of adult tool so that child can "work" alongside adult.)

Discourse Level (verbal & nonverbal)

a. Decomposition of a process: Evidence of decomposition is found in linguistic and nonlinguistic cueing of segments and boundaries between segments. These cues show that participants are breaking the process up into distinct parts:

— coordinate sequences (e.g., "do like this too;" "opa" as a marker of boundary between operations)

— subordinate sequences (e.g., X & Y are embedded in A — in order to do A, you have to do X & Y)

— suprasegmentals to mark discontinuity (e.g., stress, pauses, volume, speed of speech, intonation, pitch, etc.)

— nonverbal cues (e.g., shifts in activity or body posture, gesticulation, etc.)

b. Referring to relationships among elements of knowledge system (declarative teaching):

Knowledge systems are not decomposed in terms of steps or stages, but the system may be clarified in terms of the relationships its elements, e.g.:

— providing reasons (e.g., "it's not nice to say *em ti*")

— showing consequence (e.g.,"so as not to wet . . .)

— providing specifics to illustrate general point

— providing generalization of specifics

4. **N's Intent to learn** (learn = increase knowledge or expertise in self)

Evidence in: a. N observing or attending to E (This could probably be subsumed under "Shared Focus" because if focus is shared then N must be observing or attending to E)

b. N imitating E (Imitation can be physical, linguistic, or both)

c. N practicing (The difference between imitating and practicing is that in practice there may be no immediate model to observe, so N practices from his or her own internalized model)

d. N repeating E's telling or directive (e.g., "I press the bell hard")

e. N acting on E's telling or directive, even without E providing a physical model

f. N not showing any negative reactions to E's decomposition or contextualization (on the assumption that people will react negatively if they are told how to do (or why to do) something they already know or think they know.)

5. Evaluation

Evidence in:

a. Overt evaluation by E (e.g., "Bravo," "Good," etc.)

b. Intrinsic sign of outcome (e.g., Grandma answers doorbell)

c. Intrinsic or overt evaluation at a later time (e.g., if you are taught to do something which you will actually enact later, then evaluation (of both types) will occur after the enactment)

d. Public or institutional evaluation (e.g., Panhellenic exam results broadcast over national television; in this case there was overt evaluation at an earlier stage of preparation, culminating in the broad public evaluation after the exam)

Appendix C: Relationships Among Neighbors

#	Family Members	Kinship to #1	Other Kinship	Relational Factors
1	Grigoris & Katerina Yorgakis	—	See Families 2–10	a, b, c, d, e, f, g, h
2	Antreas† & Athanasia Yorgakis; Dimitris & Sofia Yorgakis; children Thomas & Antreas	Antreas Y. = 1st cousin to Grigoris Y; their fathers were brothers	Antreas Yorgakis is Eli Ntiroyiannis' uncle	a, b, c, d, e, f, g, h
3	Eli & Yiannis Ntiroyiannis; Vasillis & Ntida Ntiroyiannis; children Maria, Yiannis & Elena	Eli N. = niece of Grigoris Y; Eli's father was Grigoris' 1st cousin	" " " " "	a, b, c, d, h
4	Maria Makri; Agouri & Alekos Maravas; children Elenitsa & Dimitra	none	Agouri is Marta Makri's niece	a, b, c, g, h
5	Koula & Evangelos† Karagounis; Eleni & Vasilis Karagounis; children Vasoula & Vangelis	Evangelos Karagounis was Katerina's 1st cousin and Grigoris' 2nd cousin	Evangelos†, Thomas, Kostas, and Apostolis† Karagounis = 1st cousins	a, b, c, d, e, f, g, h
6	Thomas & Maria Karagounis; Eleni & Christos Skouras; child Thanasis	Thomas Karagounis = Katerina's 1st cousin & Grigoris' 2nd cousin	" " " "	a, b, c, d, e, f, g, h
7	Kostas & Chrisoula Karagounis; daughter Angela	Kostas Karagounis = Katerina's 1st cousin & Grigoris' 2nd cousin	" " " "	a, b
8	Apostolis† & Koula Karagounis; Stavros & Kitsa Ntellas; children Apostolis & Tzimas	Apostolis Karagounis = Katerina's 1st cousin & Grigoris' 2nd cousin	" " " "	a, b, c, d, e, f, g, h
9	Nikos Stragalis	Nikos = godfather of Katerina & Grigoris' daughter Noula	none	a, b
10	Marta Makri; Vasilis & Rebecca Makris; children Marta & Giorgos	Marta Makri = niece of Grigoris Yorgakis (Marta's mother & Grigoris = 1st cousins)	Marta Makri = aunt of Agouri Maravas	a, b, c

Appendix D:
Informal Teaching and
Learning Interview

Case Number _____ Date _____ Location _____

Others present _____

Birthdate _____

Residence _____

Age _____ Marital Status _____

Sex _____   Children:

Occupation _____   Age: _____ M F

Years Schooling _____   _____ M F

Yearly Income _____   _____ M F

1. a. Who brought you up? _____
   b. What did you learn from these people?
      1. _____
      2. _____
      3. _____
2. a. Can you read? _____   Write? _____
   b. If so, what kinds of things do you read?

   Write?

3. Do you know any foreign languages? If so, which ones?

   a. How do you rate your proficiency in each?

   b. Do you use these languages now? If so, for what?

   c. How did you learn these languages?

4. a. Do you speak different kinds of Greek in different situations (eg. home,
      work, shopping, etc.)?

   b. If so, what are these different kinds?

   c. How are they different?

5. How did you learn your work?

6. Have you ever been outside of Greece?
   a. If so, where?

   b. How long?

   c. For what reason(s)?

   d. How did you travel (pullman, solo, etc.)?

7. a. What behaviors show you that a child (before school age) is very smart?

   b. What behaviors show you that an adult (outside school) is very smart?

8. a. Do you ever take your child with you to work?
   b. If so, what role(s) does s/he play there?

   c. Why do you bring (or not bring) him/her?

9. What goals do you have for your children?
   M F _____
   M F _____
   M F _____
   a. Are the goals different for male and female children?
      If so, how?

10. Let's say you have a child of about ten years old, and you want to send her/him
    to *frontistirio*—How do you choose the *frontistirio*?

   a. What role do the following factors play in your decision?
      Know teacher _____
      Close to home _____
      Quality of teaching _____

11. If you could change something in the school system here in Greece (including
    frontistiria) what would you change and why?

12. a. What does the word *morfosi* mean to you?

   b. Are there different kinds of *morfosi*?
      If so, what are they?

   c. Is it possible for someone who has not had much schooling to be *morfome-nos*? _____ If so, how?

13. When you say that someone is *kathisterizmenos,* what do you mean?

14. Does the word *mangas* have a primarily positive or negative connotation?

15. a. Is it necessary to be *ponyiros* in order to survive in Greek society?

   b. If so, in which situations?

   c. How did you learn?

16. Do you know where the confectioner's shop Manolis is? _____
    Pretend that I don't know, and you are giving me directions to get there
    (Asklepiou & KTEL are references)

    (if not Manolis, use Dr.'s office)

17. Think of a distant relative of yours, and imagine that we are all at a *yorti*
    together; introduce her/him to me:

18. Let's say that I have just written a card to a pediatrician in Thessaloniki. I have
    met her only once—we had lunch together and talked mainly professionally.
    She has since sent me an article that I asked her for, and I have written this card
    to thank her. How should I end the card before signing my name?

19. Let's say that you are taking care of a small child (about 4 years old). There is
    another adult in the house, but s/he is busy at the moment. You want to go for
    five minutes to the market to get milk, but you don't want the child to know
    you're going because s/he will be upset. How do you manage to go and get the
    milk?

20. I want to learn some Greek dances. What is the best way for me to learn?

21. I am going to play for you a dialogue which I recorded. In this dialogue, you
    will hear a grandmother sewing at her machine. Her grandchild and I are
    nearby, watching. After a moment the grandfather comes in.
        Listen . . . . Now explain to me (as if I hadn't
    been there) what happened:

Appendix E:
Transcripts

Transcript of Dancing Episode

Seconds	Verbal	Nonverbal
0	G. *opa pss pss*	G clapping and singing to music
7	*Mpempi, kane kai etsi*	A dancing
	(Bebi, do like this too)	G claps hand under knee
9	A. *ti kanei ti mousiki Rosy*	A faces R
	(What makes the music Rosy)	
	G. *akou ela edho*	A faces G
	(listen come here)	G claps hand under knee
14	A. *ti kanei ti mousiki*	
	(what makes the music)	
	G. yia kane etsi	G claps hand under knee
	(hey do like this)	
15	A. *ti kanei ti mousiki*	A faces G
	(what makes the music)	
17	G. *kane kane*	G nods head, moves hand
	(do do)	A bends down, straightens
	opa	G claps hands normally
22	G. *kane kai ta palamakia*	
	(do the handclapping too)	A claps hands four times
		G and R laugh
		G rests hands on knees
		G starts clapping normally
32	A. *he ti pothara*	A claps under knee twice
	(he the big leg)	
35	G. *etsi etsi*	G claps under knee
	(like this like this)	G claps under knee
36	*etsi etsi*	
	(like this like this)	
39	*opa*	
	kane kai etsi	A still clapping under knee
	(do like this too)	G circles hands
		A circles hands, then thumbs
46	G. *ah etsi*	G circles thumbs
	(ah like that)	
47	*kane kai etsi*	A, already circling thumbs,
	(do like that too)	turns to face G
51	R. *iparhei kai afto mesa ah*	
	(there's that in it too ah)	G faces R, nods, laughs
55	G. *opa*	G moves hands out one at a time,
		rhythmically
60	*na fereis to Tsitsani*	A moves hands out one at a time,
	(bring Tsitsanis [musician])	rhythmically

Transcript of Cupping Episode

Line #	Verbal	Nonverbal
1	A. *Mpampa na'rtho ekei* (Papa shall I go there)	N. gets onto bed; A. starts out toward living room where T. is;
2	N. *ela ela tora na me pareis* *yia na figo istera na sikotho* (come come now do it so I can go afterwards to get up)	N. calls after A.
3	A. *stasou na paro ena pirouni* *(wait so I can get a fork)*	
4	N. *ela to'ho edho to'ho etimo* (come I have it here I have it ready)	
5	R. *ela Alexi* (come Alexi)	
6	N. *to'ho etima ela ohi* *fotia paidi mou ela* *as to ligo Thoma na* *paixei ligo yia na* *sikotho* *ela eho edho ela* (I have it ready come not fire my child come let him be a little Thoma to play so I can get up come I have it here come) *ela na to* (come here it is)	N lies down on bed; A and T's voices are heard in the living room A enters first, then T N shows fork with cotton to A as he enters room
7	A. *me to piroun'* (with the fork)	
8	N. *Na to* (here it is)	A takes fork in left hand, has glass in right hand
9	A. *ah ah ah*	
10	T. *etsi psemata eh* (like that play/fake eh)	
11	A. *ah nai* (ah yes)	
12	T. *endaxi* (OK)	T leans over N, lifts sweater over her back; pulls her pants down a little
13	A. *anixe to* (open it)	
14	T. *aneva edho pano* (get up here)	
15	A. *ah he he he* *(koufala?) sta Trikala* *(?) in Trikala)* *kook*	A climbs onto N's back, straddles her, pulls her pants down a little more
16	N. *stamata mi me tsadizeis* (stop it don't make me mad)	N pulls pants back up

(continued)

Transcript of Cupping Episode *(continued)*

Line #	Verbal	Nonverbal
17	T. *malak* (jerk)	T. laughs
18	N. *ante olo vlakies* (go on such nonsense)	A is astride N, with glass and fork
19	T. *vale* (put)	T stands beside A
20	N. *ante kane me* (go on do it to me)	
21	T. *ante vale* (go on put)	
22	A. *ooh ooh*	
23	T. *vale vale* (put put) *oraia vale alli* (good put another)	A inserts fork in glass, removes fork and inverts glass on N's back
24	A. *fere t'allo* (bring the other)	A. looks in direction of other glass on bed
25	T. *ela tin idia tin idia* *tin idia tin idia na ti* *valeis kai na ti vgaleis* *sinehia* (come on the same the same the same the same put it on and take it off continually)	cotton falls off of fork
26	R. *op epaize to vambaki* (oops the cotton fell off)	
27	N. (laughs)	
28	A. *eeh eeh ti fotia* (eeh eeh the fire) *fere k'allo* (bring the other)	T puts cotton back on fork; holds onto fork and cotton with A so there are 2 hands on fork A points to glass on bed
29	N. *tora edho einai par'to* (now here it is take it)	T takes glass which is already in A's hand; presses glass into N's back; still holds onto fork with A
30	T. *ante vale alli* (go on put another)	
31	A. *ase me ase ase* (leave me let go let go)	
32	T. *na min afiso to vambaki* *piase kai to vambaki* (I don't want to leg go of the cot- ton; hold on to the cotton too)	T wraps A's fingers around cotton
33	A. *nai nai nai to valo nai nai* (yes yes yes I put it yes yes)	A moves head sideways in local "yes" motion

(continued)

Transcript of Cupping Episode *(continued)*

Line #	Verbal	Nonverbal
34	T. *ante vouta to* *ah vale allo tora* *aftin tin alli pou einai* *edho aftin* *ante vale pali* (go on dip/plunge it ah put another now this one the other which is here this one go on put again)	T points to glass already on N's back
35	N. (laughs 4×)	
36	A. (makes hissing/burning noises)	A uses glasses and fork, doesn't speak; T starts to walk out of room, makes hand motion as if to say "what a mess;" laughs
37	A. *tora ezvise i fotia* (now the fire went out)	A looks up toward camera

Transcript of Babyclothes Episode

Line #	Verbal
1	S. *eidhes pos ti lene tora pou pire aera ligo* (you see how what he says now that he got a little air)
2	M. *eh kala (thelei etsi) alla krima omos* (of course he (wants it like that) but it's too bad though)
3	S. *ti krima* (what's too bad)
4	R. *krima yiati* (too bad why)
5	S. *mono otan ( ) otan t'allazeis dhen eh's ena kati etsi san auto yia na min katourisei as poume* (only when ( ) when you change him don't you have a something like that so that he won't urinate shall we say)
6	E. *nai more eho alla to eho sto krevati tora katalaves to eho mesa* (yes dear I have but I have it in the bed now understand, I have it inside)
7	M. *ehei sto krebati* (she has in the bed)
8	E. *thelo na paro allo* (I want to get another)
9	S. *na toh's edho pera* (you should have it here)
10	M. *dhen tha to val's ziponaki* (aren't you going to put an undershirt on him)
11	E. *dhen to forao ziponaki* (I don't put an undershirt on him)
12	S. *as to etsi ligo asto na paizei ( )* (leave him like that a little let him play)
13	M. *ohi ohi ohi ohi val'to* (no no no no put it on)
14	S. *asto mari na parei aera to paidhi* (let him be dear to get some air, the child)
15	M. *ohi na valei tin tetoia ti* (no she should put on the thing, the)
16	S. *etsi Theia einai pio kala* *(like this, Aunt, it's better)*
17	M. *kala tora ( ) avrio* *(good for now ( ) tomorrow*
18	E. *(. . .) na katourisei to stroma edho tha mirizei katourila hm* (. . .) to urinate on the mattress here it will smell of urine hmm) (laughs)
19	S. *nai na to vazeis vraki mono na min to vazei mpempilino na tafin's etsi na paizei* (yes you should put on his panties only don't put on "Babylino" leave him like this to play)
20	E. *me ta podharakia* (with his little legs)
21	S. *Nai* (yes)
22	E. *kala les ego dhen ton eho foresei katholou ektos apo Pampers pote kilotaki* (you're right I haven't put anything but "Pampers" on him never panties)
23	S. *dhen ton eh's kilotakia* (don't you have panties for him)

(*continued*)

Transcript of Babyclothes Episode (continued)

Line #	Verbal
24	E. *(tin ehoume?) vevaia ehoume* (we have it?) of course we have it
25	S. *hm kilotakia mono* (hmm only panties)
26	M. *ehoume ( ) yemata* (we have ( ) full)
27	E. *kai auta apo'dho pera ola* (and these from here all)
28	S. *hmm vrakaki mono na min halasei kai ta Mpempilino pou ehoun trianta dhrahmes to ena hmm (yelaei)* (hmm panties only so you won't waste the "Babylino" which cost thirty drachmas each hmm (laughs))
29	R. *kala afto dhen to les Mpempilino* (isn't this what you call "Babylino")
30	S. *nai afto einai* (yes that's it)
31	E. *nai* (yes)
32	R. *Pampers*
33	S. *auto einai ap'ta kala iparhei* (that's the good kind there's)
34	R. *to megalo pou les* (the big one you mean)
35	S. *iparhoun kai Mpempilino nai einai ama per's as poume yia pio oikonomia ama to vazei afta ta alla ta sketa apo kato pou einai opos einai ta'fta paidhi mou tis sketes tis panes opos ehoume tis servietes* (there's Babylino yes it's if you get shall we say to save money if you put on these others the plain ones underneath which are like those my dear the plain ones the cloth like we have sanitary napkins)
36	R. *hmmm*
37	E. *aa nai* (oh yes)
38	S. *katalaves* (you see)
39	E. *alla ekeinone ti einai mesa se kilotaki ee* (but those what are they inside the panties eh)
40	S. *nai tha to vazei ekeino opos vazoume emeis kai tha vazeis kai to kilotaki apo pano* (yes you'll put that as we put ours and you'll put the panties on top)
41	E. *hmm katalava* (hmm I see)
42	S. *kala ti nihta vevaia ama the's na mi mouskevei na mi ftiahnei einao pio kala afto para ekeino* (Of course at night if you don't want him to get wet to make it's better to use this rather than that (baby makes small sounds)) *alla etsi yia ti mera ekeino prepei na einai pio fthino ( ) pio oikonomiko* (but for the day that must be cheaper ( ) more economical)
43	E. *ekeino einai Mpempilino pou einai sa servieta* (that's Babylino which is like a sanitary napkin)

(continued)

Transcript of Babyclothes Episode (*continued*)

Line #	Verbal
44	S. *yiati Mpempilino dhen ehoun tetoia ehoun kai tetoia kai Mpempilino* (why, doesn't Babylino have those they have those in Babylino too)
45	E. *sa Pampers* (like Pampers)
46	S. *ehoun kai tetoia Mpempilino paidhi mou opos einai afto ehoun kai* (they have those in Babylino too my dear like this they have too)
47	E. *dhen xero pana vrakaki ta mperdevo re paidi mou einai* (I don't know overpanties I get them confused my dear it's)
48	S. *koita afto einai pana vrakaki se Pampers pana vrakaki iparhei se Mpempilino* (look this is an overpanty in Pampers you can get the overpanty in Babylino)
49	E. *ah ah*
50	S. *prepei na iparhei kai Mpempilino iparhei kai diafores markes as poume kata-* *laves pou'nai pana vrakaki* (Babylino must make one too there are several different brands shall we say you see which are overpanties)
51	E. *dhen to'xera* (I didn't know that)
52	S. *alla iparhei as poume kai prepei na iparhei kai Pampers sketo tetoio dhen* *xero an iparhei Pampers alla t'alla iparhoun diafora einai polles markes* (but there are shall we say and there must be also plain Pampers like this I don't know if there are Pampers but the others exist several there are many brands)
53	E. *nai einai polla nai* (yes there are many yes)
54	S. *kane me mama pes na paro ligo aerako sta potharakia* (make me Mama say to get a little air on my legs) [babytalk as if Soula were baby]
55	E. *o Antreas dhen milaei the ton milaei katholou to mpempi eh* (Andreas doesn't talk he doesn't talk to him at all the baby eh)
56	S. ( ) *milaei* ( ) talks
57	E. *dhen to milaei katholou pou pigate Antrea me to karo pou piges* (he doesn't talk to him at all where did you go Andreas with the cart where did you go)
58	A. *edho pera* (around here)
	**********
	(baby makes noises)
59	E. *ti e* (what eh (laughing))
60	S. *hairetai e olo hares einai* (he's happy eh he's all gladness)
61	E. ( ) *e edho sta podhia na to foreso omos kati (etho kati)* (laughing) ( ) eh here on his feet I should put something though)
62	A. *ego leo na to foreseis leptes kaltses* (I say you should put thin socks on him)
63	E. *leptes kaltses leptes kaltses thelei o Antreas* (thin socks (laughing) thin socks Andreas wants) *plaka tha ehei o pateras tou* (his father will be amused)

(*continued*)

Transcript of Babyclothes Episode (*continued*)

Line #	Verbal
64	S. ( ) *ihai otan tharthei o pateras tou tha koimatai o mpempis* ( ) (oh boy when his father comes the baby will be sleeping)
65	E. *ohi ( )* (no ( ))
66	R. *tis erhomenes meres pou tha ton vlepei* (the next days when he sees him)
67	S. *kala einai autos ti zitaei me to poukamisaki kai dhen foraei to ti kapa pou forouse to heimona* (he's good now what does he want with the little shirt and he doesn't wear the the cap that he wore in winter)
68	R. hmm
69	S. *kai forese ta kalokairina kai evgale kai ti flanela* (and he wore summer clothes and took off the undershirt)
70	E. *foraei ap'afta ta lepta ta kalokairina e mpempi* (he wears the light ones the summer ones right Bebi)
71	S. ( )
72	E. *einai kai thalassia kai afta me aspro* (they're light blue those with white)
73	R. *oraio* (nice)
74	E. *vevaia ola asorti* (you bet all coordinated)
75	S. *m'eskases re Mama pes m'evales kai tis dio tis kouvertes* (you suffocated me Mama tell her you put both blankets over me)
76	E. ( ) *pani* ( ) cloth
77	S. *tis heimoniatikes ( )* (the winter ones ( )) *m'evales kai tis hondres tis formes* (you made me wear the heavy jumpsuits too)
78	A. *to vgazei to Mpempilino* (he's taking off the Babylino (laughs))
79	E. Ha (laughs)
	************
80	E. *pineis to gala mpempi e* (you're drinking the milk, Bebi eh)
81	R. *se yelasame e* (we fooled you eh)
82	E. *mm pineis to gala* (mmm you're drinking the milk)
83	A. ha (laughs)
84	E. *se yelasame me tin pipila dhen tin pairnei panta tin pipila opote thelei* (we fooled you with the pacifier he doesn't always take it the pacifier just when he wants)
85	S. *kalitera min tin ego dhen piran pote afta dhen tin epairnan me to zori koita einai idhromeno mouskema* (better not to I they never took those they didn't used to use them even if I forced them to look he's sweating all wet (the baby makes noises))
86	E. *eidika hthes to vradi dhen mporouse na koimithei to paidhi na einai to kefali tou olo vregmeno* (especially last night he couldn't sleep the child so wet was his head)

(*continued*)

Transcript of Babyclothes Episode (*continued*)

Line #	Verbal
87	S. *em istera pos perimenes na koimithei pos perimenes na koimithei kat'arhin* *otan otan idhronei tin petaei kai tin kouverta kai kathetai me to* (so how do you expect him to sleep how do you expect him to sleep first of all when when he sweats he throws the cover off and stays like that with the)
88	R. *opos kaname prin* (like we did before)
89	S. *e vevaia afto to etsi na poume to peis pou xereis to paidhi as poume ti thelei* *alla ligo poli paradheigmatizetai o allos ap'ton eafto tou opos dinesai esi na* *prospathisei na dineis kai to paidhi as poume afou esi dhen krioneis paei na* *pi oti oute to paidhi tha krionei* (eh of course this like this we might say you say who knows what the child wants but more or less one can use oneself as an example as you dress your- self so should you try to dress the child, so to speak since you're not cold it means that neither the child will get cold) (baby makes noises)
90	E. *iha ehei eikosiexi vathmous mesa m'anoikta ola ti hara mou theleis na fas* *theleis e theleis* (I had it's twenty-six degrees inside with everything open what my joy do you want to eat do you want eh do you want)
91	S. ( ) *Antrea apo dho thelei galataki na faei tora* (( ) Andreas from here he wants to eat milk now)
92	A. hmm
93	E. *pou einai o Antreas pou einai irthe o Antreas e* (where's Andreas where is he Andreas came eh)

Transcript of Kinship Episode

Line #	Verbal
1	A. *ah agk yiati esi ti les mama* (ah agk why do you call her mama)
2	R. Hmm
3	A. *ah yiati* (ah why)
4	K. *mama dhen m'ehei* (doesn't she have me as mama)
5	A. *nai yiati eisai mama* (yes why are you a mama)
6	K. *eimai mama dhen eimai mama* (I'm a mama aren't I a mama)
7	A. *ohi* (no)
8	K. *ti eimai* (what am I)
9	A. *yiayia eisai* (you're a grandma)
10	K. *yiayia eimai yia sena* (grandma I am for you)
11	A. *yia ti Rosy* (for Rosy)
12	K. *yia ti Rosy eimai mama* (for Rosy I am a mama)
13	A. *yiati* (why)
14	K. *etsi mama dhen eimai* (like that aren't I a mama)
15	A. *i giki mou i mama* (My own mother/Kiki's mother) [due to A's mispronunciation of *dhiki mou* (my own mother), K hears *Kiki mou,* which is A's sister]
16	K. *i Kiki sou dhen ehei mama* (doesn't your Kiki have a mother)
17	A. *kai sena se leei kai mama* (she calls you mama too)
18	K. *i Kiki me leei yiayia pos na pei mama ehei ti Nina* (Kiki calls me grandma what she has Nina as mama)
19	A. *nai ti ti ti mama mou pos* (yes the the the my mama how)
20	K. *ti mama sou* (your mama)
21	A. *ti ti mama mou pos ti leei ti mama mou pos* (the the my mama how does she call her my mama how)
22	K. *pios* (who)
23	A. *i Rosy pos ti leei ti mama mou* (Rosy how does she call my mama)
24	K. *ni Nina*
25	A. *pos yia* (how)

(continued)

Transcript of Kinship Episode (*continued*)

Line #	Verbal
26	K. *pos na tin pei* (how should she call her)
27	A. *na na ti leei yiayia* (she should should call her grandma)
28	K. *yiayia einai i mama s'* (is your mother a grandma)
29	R. hmm
30	K. *re Alexi yiati mas ta perdheveis* (hey Alexi why do you mix it up for us)
31	A. *dhen einai yiayia i* (isn't she a grandmother)
32	R. *xereis pote tha einai yiayia* (do you know when she'll be a grandma)
33	K. ha (laughs)
34	R. *otan kanei i Rena kai i Kiki* (when Rena and Kiki make)
35	K. moro (a baby)
36	R. *kai si mora tote tha einai yiayia prepei na kanei ta dhika tis paidheia paidheia katalaves* (and you babies then she will be a grandma her children must have children understand)
37	A. *nai katalava kai 'go sa yino mm siga to homa* (yes I understood and I will become mm careful of the earth)

Transcript of *Em ti* Episode

Line #	Verbal
1	A. *ase me* (leave me alone)
2	G. *ftiase dhromo* (make a road)
3	A. ( )
4	G. *aftos dhen einai kalos dhromos dhen pernan t'aftokinita pernan ta trakteria* *( ) etsi* (that's not a good road cars don't pass on it tractors pass ( ) right)
5	A. *em ti kanoun dhen pernan* (what do you think they do don't they pass)
6	T. *na to pali Alexi ti eipes tora* (there it is again Alexi what did you just say)
7	G. *pos eipes tora ti kanoun* (how did you say now what do they do)
8	K. (laughs)
9	R. *em ti*
10	A. *dhen pernan ta trakteria* (tractors don't pass)
11	G. *dhen pernoun* (they don't pass) [different pronunciation]
12	T. *ela tora min allazeis ( ) eisai poli ponyiros* (come on now don't change ( ) you're very clever)
13	K. *em ti kanoun kai dhen pernan* (what do they do don't they pass)
14	T. *eisai dhiplomatis tora min allazeis kouvenda ti eipes proigoumenos* (you're a diplomat now don't change the topic what did you say before)
15	K. *vre Toni dhen boreis na antimetopeis afto to pragma* (hey Toni you can't do anything about that thing)
16	T. *ego Alexi ti sou eipa* (I Alexi what did I say to you)
17	A. Hmm
18	T. *ti sou eipa* [whispers] (what did I tell you)
19	A. *ot-* (that-)
20	T. *mi me kittas emena ponyira* (don't look at me cleverly)
21	A. *to em ti dhen einai kalo* (the *em ti* is not good)
22	T. *dhen einai dhen einai kalo dhen einai oraio* (it's not that it isn't good it isn't nice)
23	A. ( )
24	T. *mi me kittas emena etsi ah ponyira* (don't look at me like that ah cleverly)
25	A. ( )
26	T. *ma pos me kittas ponyira* (but of course you're looking at me cleverly)
27	K. *(exoda [?])* (exit [?])

(continued)

Transcript of *Em ti* Episode (*continued*)

Line #	Verbal
28	T. *kitta edho na to etsi me kittas ponyira ah to vlepo* (look here there it is like that you're looking at me cleverly I see it)
29	K. ( ) *kourepse ta mallia tou ap'kato anagastika i mana sou tha ta ftiaxei istera* ( ) (if his hair is cut from the bottom necessarily your mother will fix it afterwards)
30	T. *vlepeis* (do you see)
31	G. *einai oraios* (he's good)
31	K. *ah mare papse* (oh you stop it)
32	G. ( )
33	A. *dhen eipa to em ti dhen to eipa* (I didn't say the *em ti* I didn't say it)
34	T. *mi mou les psemata to eipes* (don't tell me lies you said it)
35	A. *dhen to eipa an me leen psemata* ( ) (I didn't say it if they tell me lies ( ))
36	G. *dhen mou les Alexandre Alexandre tha pame sto potami* (won't you tell me Alexander Alexander shall we go to the river)
37	A. *em ti*
38	G. *aaap*
39	K. *ha haaa*
40	T. *ti eipes tora [laughs] tora ti eipes* (what did you say now [laughs] now what did you say)
41	G. *pali ta idia* (again the same)
42	T. *pes nai tha pame sto potami yiati les em ti* (say "yes we'll go to the river" why do you say *em ti*)
43	K. ah hah
44	T. *nai tha pame i ohi dhen tha pame* ("yes we'll go" or "no we won't go")
45	A. *tha pao tha po* [very quiet] ("I'll go" I'll say)
46	T. *bravo*
47	K. *sou po* ( ) (tell you ( ))
47	G. *eh tha paroume kai psomi eh* (eh we need to get bread too)

Transcript of *Trapezi* Episode

Line #	Verbal
1	K. *ego t'Alexi leo tapezi*
	(I'm Alexis and I say "tapezi") [*tapezi* = mispronunciation of *trapezi* (table)]
2	A. *ohi*
	(no)
3	K. *Esi pos to les*
	(how do you say it)
4	A. *Yiayioula le selo na yineis mikri*
	(Grandma I don't want you to become little)
5	K. *na'mai megali*
	(should I be big)
6	A. *nai*
	(yes)
7	K. *kai pos na leo yia pes to 'si*
	(and how should I say it you say it)
8	A. *Yiayia nen efages akoma*
	(Grandma didn't you eat yet)
9	K. *nai efaga tora trapezi*
	(yes I just ate *trapezi* (table))
10	A. *ah ah Yiayia*
	(ah ah Grandma)
11	K. *Nai*
	(yes)
12	A. *ti eipes*
	(what did you say)
13	K. *yia pes to kai 'si*
	(you say it too)
14	A. *trapez' eipes*
	(*trapez* you said)
15	K. *trapezi*
	(*trapezi* (table))
16	A. *aa ti einai pos efages ki'ola kai megaloses toso gigora re Yiayia*
	(ah what is it how did you eat and all and grow big so quickly Grandma)
17	K. *kaleka*
	(chair) (mispronounced)
18	K. *nai kaleta*
	(yes *kaleta* (chair mispronounced))
19	A. *fai re Yiayioula*
	(eat Grandma)
20	K. *pos to lene yia pes*
	(how do they say it you say)
21	A. *karekla*
	(*karekla* (chair, correct pronunciation)
22	K. Aaa
23	A. *ah kaleka*
	(ah *kaleka* (chair, mispronounced)
24	K. *ohi kaleta*
	(not *kaleta* (chair, mispronounced)
25	A. *ah tora eyina mikros toukou toukou touk touk touk* . . .
	(ah now I became little tukou tukou tuk tuk tuk (tractor noises) . . .)

(continued)

Transcript of *Trapezi* Episode (*continued*)

Line #		Verbal
26	K.	*trakteri yia pes to* (tractor say it)
27	A.	*trater* (*trater* (tractor, mispronounced))
28	K.	*aaa trateri* (ah *trateri* (tractor, mispronounced))
29	A.	afto ti einai t'ein'afto Yiayia (this is what what's this Grandma)
30	K.	*trakter* (tractor)
31	R.	*elikoptero* (helicopter)
32	A.	*ohi elikoptero* (not a helicopter) (everybody laughs)
33	K.	*aaa elikoptero ee* (ah helicopter eh)
34	A.	*ohi elikoptero tater* (not a helicopter *tater* (tractor mispronounced))
35	K.	*tateri ohi tat trakteri* (*tateri* not *tat trakteri* (correct pronunciation))
36	A.	*af ekane horafi tora* (af it plowed a field now)
37	K.	*nai* (yes)
38	A.	*tora pou paei tora* (now where's it going now)
39	K.	*tora tha paai'n sto spiti tou* (now it will go (dialect form) to its house)

References

Au, K & Mason, J. (1983). Cultural congruence in classroom participation structures: Achieving a balance of rights. *Discourse Processes,6*, 145–167.

Bakhtin, M. M. (1981). *The dialogic imagination.* Austin, TX: University of Texas Press.

Bakhtin, M. M. (1986). *Speech genres and other late essays.* Austin, TX: University of Texas Press.

Banks, J., & Banks, C. (Eds.). (1989). *Multicultural education.* Boston: Allyn & Bacon.

Bateson, G. (1972). *Steps to an ecology of mind.* New York: Ballantine Books.

Benedict, R. (1934). *Patterns of culture.* Boston: Houghton Mifflin.

Boissevain, J. (1974). *Friends of friends: Networks, manipulators, and coalitions.* Oxford: Basil Blackwell.

Brown, G. & Yule, G. (1983). *Discourse analysis.* New York: Cambridge University Press.

Bruner, J. S. (1978). The role of dialogue in language acquisition. In A. Sinclair, R. J. Jarvella, & W. J. M. Levelt (Eds.), *The child's conception of language* (pp. 241–256). New York: Springer Verlag.

Burton, R., Brown, J. S., & Fischer, G. (1984). Skiing as a model of instruction. In B. Rogoff & J. Lave (Eds.), *Everyday cognition: Its development in social context* (pp. 137–150). Cambridge, MA: Harvard University Press.

Campbell, J. K. (1964). *Honour, family, and patronage: A study of institutions and moral values in a Greek mountain community.* New York: Oxford University Press.

Carroll, J. B. (1968). On learning from being told. *Educational Psychologist 5*(2),1–10.

Coleman, J. (1987). Families and schools. *Educational Researcher,16*, 32–38.

Cowan, J. K. (1990). *Dance and the body politic in northern Greece.* Princeton, NJ: Princeton University Press.

Delgado-Gaitan, C. (1987). Traditions and transitions in the learning process of Mexican children: An ethnographic view. In G. Spindler, & L. Spindler (Eds.), *Interpretive ethnogrpahy of education: At home and abroad* (pp. 333–359). Hillsdale, NJ: Lawrence Erlbaum Associates.

Dickinson, D. K. (1985). Creating and using formal occasions in the classroom. *Anthropology and Education Quarterly, 16*, 47–62.

DuBoulay, J. (1974). *Portrait of a Greek mountain village.* Oxford: Clarendon Press.

Erickson, F. (1982). Money tree, lasagna bush, salt and pepper: Social construction of topical cohesion in a conversation among Italian-Americans. In D. Tannen (Ed.), *Analyzing discourse: Text and talk* (pp. 43–69). Washington, DC: Georgetown University Press.

Erickson, F. (1986a). Qualitative research on teaching. In M.C. Wittrock (Ed.), *Handbook of research on teaching* (3rd ed., pp. 119–161). New York: MacMillan.

Erickson, F. (1986b). Tasks in times: Objects of study in a natural history of teaching. In K. K. Zumwalt (Ed.), *Improving teaching: 1986 ASCD yearbook* (pp. 131–147). Alexandria, VA: Association for Supervision and Curriculum Development.

Erickson, F. (1987). Transformation and school success: The politics and culture of educational achievement. *Anthropology and Education Quarterly 18* (4), 335–356.

Frake, C. O. (1962). The ethnographic study of cognitive systems. In T. Gladwin & W. Sturtevant (Eds.), *Anthropology and human behavior* (pp. 72–85). Washington DC: Anthropological Society of Washington.

Friedl, E. (1962). *Vasilika: A village in modern Greece.* New York: Holt, Rinehart & Winston.

Gardner, H. (1985). *Frames of mind: The theory of multiple intelligences.* New York: Basic Books.

Garfinkel, H. (1967). *Studies in ethnomethodology.* New Jersey: Prentiss-Hall.

Geertz, C. (1973). *The interpretation of cultures.* New York: Basic Books.

Gilmore, D. D. (Ed.) 1987. *Honor and shame and the unity of the Mediterranean.* Washington, DC: American Anthropological Association Special Publication, no. 22.

Gilmore, P. (1983). Spelling "Mississippi": Recontextualizing a literacy-related speech event. *Anthropology and Education Quarterly 14* (4), 235–255.

Givon, T. (1983). Topic continuity in discourse. In T. Givon (Ed.), *Topic continuity in discourse* (pp. 1–42). Amsterdam: John Benjamins.

Gladwin, T. (1970). *East is a big bird: Navigation and logic on Puluwat Atoll.* Cambridge, MA: Harvard University Press.

Goffman, E. (1974). *Frame analysis: An essay on the organization of experience.* Boston: Northeastern University Press.

Golde, P. (1986). Introduction. In P. Golde (Ed.), *Women in the field: Anthropological experiences* (pp. 1–15). Berkeley, CA: University of California Press.

Goodenough, W. H. (1957). Cultural anthropology and linguistics. In. P. Garvin (Ed.), *Report of the Seventh Annual Round Table Meeting in Linguistics and Language Study: Monograph Series on Language and Linguistics #9* (pp. 167–173). Washington, DC: Georgetown University.

Greenfield, P. (1984). A theory of the teacher in the learning activities of everyday life. In B. Rogoff & J. Lave (Eds.), *Everyday cognition: Its development in social context* (pp. 116–138). Cambridge, MA: Harvard University Press.

Gumperz, J. J. (1982). *Discourse strategies.* New York: Cambridge University Press.

Heath, S. B. (1983). *Ways with words: Language, life and work in communities and classrooms.* New York: Cambridge University Press.

Heath, S. B. (1989). The learner as cultural member. In R. Schiefelbusch & M. Rice (Eds.), *The Teachability of Language* (pp. 333–350). Baltimore, MD: P. H. Brookes.

Herzfeld, M. (1980). Honour and shame: Problems in the analysis of moral systems. *Man, 15*, 339–351.

Hess, D. (1989). Teaching ethnographic writing: A review essay. *Anthropology and Education Quarterly, 20* (3), 163–176.

Hymes, D. (1964). Introduction: Toward ethnographies of communication. In J. Gumperz & D. Hymes (Eds.), *The Ethnography of Communication,* Special Publication of *American Anthropologist, 66.6*(2), 1–34.

Hymes, D. (1972). Foundations of discourse analysis. In J. Gumperz & D. Hymes (Eds.), *Directions in Sociolinguistics: The ethnography of communication* (pp. 35–71). Oxford: Basil Blackwell.

Irvine, J. T. (1979). Formality and informality in communicative events. *American Anthropologist, 81*, 773–790.

John, V. (1972). Styles of learning, styles of teaching. In C. Cazden, V. John & D. Hymes (Eds.), *Functions of language in the classroom* (pp. 331–343). New York: Teacher's College Press.

LaBelle, T. (1984). Liberation, development, and rural nonformal education. *Anthropology and Education Quarterly, 15*, 80–93.

Lave, J. (1982). A comparative approach to educational forms and learning processes. *Anthropology and Education Quarterly, 13* (2), 181–187.

Lave, J. (1988). *Cognition in practice: Mind, mathematics and culture in everyday life.* New York: Cambridge University Press.

Leichter, H. J. (1979). Families and communities as educators: Some concepts of relationship. In H. Leichter (Ed.), *Families and communities as educators* (pp. 1–74). New York: Teachers College Press.

Leont'ev, A. N. (1979). The problem of activity in psychology: An introduction. In J. Wertsch (Ed.), *The concept of activity in Soviet psychology,* (pp. 37–71). New York: Sharpe.

Levin, P. F. (1990). Culturally contextualized apprenticeship: Teaching and learning through helping in Hawaiian families. *Quarterly Newsletter of the Laboratory of Comparative Human Cognition, 12*(2), 80–85.

Levinson, S. (1983). *Pragmatics.* New York: Cambridge University Press.

Mackridge, P. (1985). *The modern Greek language.* Oxford: Oxford University Press.

Marshall, M. & Barritt, L. (1990). Choices made, worlds created: The rhetoric of AERJ. *American Educational Research Journal, 27* (4), 589–609.

McNall, S. (1974). *The Greek peasant.* Washington DC: American Sociological Association.

Mehan, H. (1979). *Learning lessons: Social organization in the classroom.* Cambridge, MA: Harvard University Press.

Mercouri, M. (1988). Melina: Madame minister (Interview by Barbara Fields). *Aegean Review, 4*, 20–28.

Metraux, R. (1953). Resonance in imagery. In M. Mead and R. Metraux (Eds.), *The study of culture at a distance* (pp. 343–362). Chicago: University of Chicago Press.

Michaels, S. & Collins, J. (1984). Oral discourse styles: Classroom interaction and the acquisition of literacy. In D. Tannen (Ed.), *Coherence in spoken and written discourse* (pp. 219–244). Norwood, NJ: Ablex.

Michaels, S. & Cook-Gumperz, J. (1979). A study of sharing time with first grade students: Discourse narratives in the classroom. *Proceedings of the Fifth Annual Meetings of the Berkeley Linguistics Society.*

Miller, M. & Hutchins, E. (1982). *On the acquisition of boardsailing skill.* Unpublished manuscript.

Milroy, L. (1980). *Language and social networks.* Oxford: Basil Blackwell.

Ochs, E. (1982). Talking to children in Western Samoa. *Language in Society, 11*, 77–104.

Ogbu, J. U. (1978). *Minority education and costs: The American system in cross-cultural perspective.* New York: Academic Press.

Oller, J. W. & Oller, J. W. Jr. (1983). An integrated pragmatic curriculum: A Spanish program. In J. Oller Jr. & P. Richard-Amato (Eds.), *Methods that work: A smorgasbord of ideas for language teachers.* (pp. 20–37). Rowley, MA: Newbury House.

Papadimou, I. C. (1980). *I Thessali Karagounides: Mia erevna tis istorias tous kai tis laografias tous* (The Thessalian Karagounides: A study of their history and folklore). Athens: P. & S. Mangou, O. E.

Peristiany, J. (1966). Honour and shame in a Cypriot highland village. In J. Peristiany (Ed.), *Honour and Shame: The Values of Mediterranean Society* (pp. 175–190). Chicago: University of Chicago Press.

Philips, S. (1972). Participant structures and communicative competence. In C. Cazden, V.

John & D. Hymes (Eds.), *Functions of language in the classroom* (pp. 370-394). New York: Teacher's College Press.

Piestrup, J. (1973). *Black dialect interference and accomodation of reading instruction in first grade* (Monograph No. 4). Berkeley, Ca: Language-Behavior Research Laboratory.

Pratt, M. L. (1986). Fieldwork in common places. In J. Clifford & G. Marcus (Eds.), *Writing culture* (pp. 27-50). Berkeley: University of California Press.

Pring, J. T. (1982). *The Oxford Dictionary of Modern Greek*. Oxford, England: Clarendon Press.

Quinn, N. & Holland, D. (1987). Culture and cognition. In D. Holland & N. Quinn (Eds.), *Cultural Models in Language and Thought* (pp. 3-42). New York: Cambridge University Press.

Ruiz, N. T. (1988). *Language for learning in a bilingual special education classroom*. Unpublished doctoral dissertation, Stanford University, Stanford, CA.

Ryle, G. (1963). Formal and informal logic. In R. Jager (Ed.), *Essays in logic* (pp. 166-180). Englewood Cliffs, N.J.: Prentiss Hall.

Sapir, E. (1949). *Culture, language and personality*. Berkeley, CA: University of California Press.

Schieffelin, B. (1979). Getting it together: An ethnographic approach to the study of the development of communicative competence. In E. Ochs & B. Schieffelin (Eds.), *Developmental pragmatics* (pp. 73-108). New York: Academic Press.

Scollon, R. & Scollon, S. (1981). *Narrative, literacy and face in interethnic communication*. Norwood, NJ: Ablex.

Scollon, R. & Scollon, S. (1984). Cooking it up and boiling it down: Abstracts in Athabaskan children's story retellings. In D. Tannen, (Ed.), *Coherence in spoken and written discourse* (pp. 173-197). Norwood, NJ: Ablex.

Searle, J. R. (1976). A classification of illocutionary acts. *Language in Society, 5*, 1-23.

Shultz, J. & Theophano, J. (1985). *Locating learning in family interaction: An examination of dinner time in Italian-American homes*. Unpublished manuscript.

Sivignon, M. (1976). Frontier between two cultural areas: The case of Thessaly. In M. Dimen & E. Friedl (Eds.), *Regional variation in modern Greece and Cyprus: Toward a perspective on the ethnography of Greece* (pp. 43-58). Annals of the New York Academy of Sciences. 268.

Skinner, B. F. (1938). *The behavior of organisms: An experimental analysis*. New York: Appleton-Century-Crofts.

Tannen, D. (1984). Spoken and written narrative in English and Greek. In D. Tannen (Ed.), *Coherence in spoken and written discourse* (pp. 21-24). Nowrood, NJ: Ablex.

Van Dijk, T. (1982). Episodes as units of discourse analysis. In D. Tannen (Ed.), *Analyzing discourse: Text and talk* (pp. 177-195). Washington, DC: Goergetown University Press.

Varenne, H. & McDermott, R. (1986). "Why" Shiela can read: Structure and indeterminacy in the reproduction of familial literacy. In B. Schieffelin & P. Gilmore (Eds.), *The acquisition of literacy: Ethnographic perspectives* (pp. 188-210). Norwood, NJ: Ablex.

Vygotsky, L. (1962). *Thought and language*. Cambridge, MA: MIT Press.

Vygotsky, L. (1978). *Mind in society*. Cambridge, MA: Harvard University Press.

Wallace, A. (1961). Schools in revolutionary and conservative societies. In F. Gruber (Ed.), *Anthropology and education* (pp. 25-54). Philadelphia: University of Pennsylvania Press.

Werner, O. (1985). Folk knowledge without the fuzz. In J. W. D. Dougherty (Ed.), *Directions in cognitive anthropology* (pp. 73-90). Chicago: University of Illinois Press.

Whorf, B. (1956). *Language, thought, and reality*. Cambridge, MA: MIT Press.

Wolcott, H. (1982). The anthropology of learning. *Anthropology and Education Quarterly, 13*(2), 83-108.

Zinchenko, P.I. (1979). Involuntary memory and the goal-directed nature of activity. J. V. Wertsch (Ed.), *The concept of activity in Soviet psychology* (pp. 72-88). New York: Sharpe.

Author Index

Subject Index